DEFEND YOURSELF AGAINST CRIMINAL CHARGES

DEFEND YOURSELF AGAINST CRIMINAL CHARGES

Michael Saeger
Attorney at Law

Sourcebooks
Inc.

Naperville, IL • Clearwater, FL

Published by: **Sourcebooks, Inc.**

Naperville Office
P.O. Box 372
Naperville, Illinois 60566
(630) 961-3900
FAX: 630-961-2168

Clearwater Office
P.O. Box 25
Clearwater, Florida 33757
(813) 587-0999
FAX: 813-586-5088

Cover Design: Andrew Sardina/Dominique Raccah
Interior Design and Production: Andrew Sardina, Sourcebooks, Inc.

This publication is designed to provide accurate and authoritative information in regard to the subject matter covered. It is sold with the understanding that the publisher is not engaged in rendering legal, accounting, or other professional service. If legal advice or other expert assistance is required, the services of a competent professional person should be sought.
From a Declaration of Principles Jointly Adopted by a Committee of the American Bar Association and a Committee of Publishers and Associations

Library of Congress Cataloging-in-Publication Data
Saeger, Michael, 1948-
  Defend yourself against criminal charges / Michael Saeger.
    p. cm.
  Includes index.
  ISBN 1-57071-162-3 (pbk.)
  1. Criminal procedure — United States — Popular works. 2. Defense (Criminal procedure) — United States — Popular works. I. Title.
KF9619.6.S24   1997
345.73'05—dc21   97-22838
                                                                                                                      CIP

Printed and bound in the United States of America.

Paperback — 10 9 8 7 6 5 4 3 2 1

For my mother, whose common sense advice to me was always better than any legal advice I gave anybody else.

Contents

ACKNOWLEDGMENTS

I'd like to thank Laurie Johnson, who's been a loyal and very efficient secretary for many years. She typed most of the first drafts of this book. I'd like to thank my son, Chuck, as well. He did a first-rate job of editing out his old man's "legalese."

Most of all, I'd like to thank my many clients, who have often been the recipients of my mistakes and occasionally of my genius. The advice and explanations I routinely give to a client form the backbone of this book. I wish them all well—both the not guilty and the not quite so not guilty.

Using Self-Help Law Books

Whenever you shop for a product or service, you are faced with various levels of quality and price. In deciding what product or service to buy, you make a cost/value analysis on the basis of your willingness to pay and the quality you desire.

When buying a car, you decide whether you want transportation, comfort, status, or sex appeal. Accordingly, you decide among such choices as a Neon, a Lincoln, a Rolls Royce, or a Porsche. Before making a decision, you usually weigh the merits of each option against the cost.

When you get a headache, you can take a pain reliever (such as aspirin) or go visit a medical specialist for a neurological examination. Given this choice, most people, of course, take a pain reliever, since it costs only pennies, whereas a medical examination costs hundreds of dollars and takes a lot of time. This is usually a logical choice because rarely is anything more than a pain reliever needed for a headache. But in some cases, a headache may indicate a brain tumor, and failing to see a specialist right away can result in complications. Should everyone with a headache go to a specialist? Of course not, but people treating their own illnesses must realize that they are betting on the basis of their cost/value analysis of the situation, they are taking the most logical option.

The same cost/value analysis must be made in deciding to do one's own legal work. Many legal situations are very straightforward, requiring a simple form and no complicated analysis. Anyone with a little intelligence and a book of instructions can handle the matter without outside help.

But there is always the chance that complications are involved that only an attorney would notice. To simplify the law into a book like this, several legal cases often must be condensed into a single sentence or paragraph. Otherwise, the book would be several hundred pages long and too complicated for most people. However, this simplification necessarily leaves out many details and nuances that would apply to special or unusual situations. Also, there are many ways to interpret most legal questions. Your case may come before a judge who disagrees with the analysis of our authors.

Therefore, in deciding to use a self-help law book and to do your own legal work, you must realize that you are making a cost/value analysis and deciding that the chance your case will not turn out to your satisfaction is outweighed by the money you will save in doing it yourself. Most people handling their own simple legal matters never have a problem, but occasionally people find that it ended up costing them more to have an attorney straighten out the situation than it would have if they had hired an attorney in the beginning. Keep this in mind while handling your case, and be sure to consult an attorney if you feel you might need further guidance.

INTRODUCTION

WHO IS THIS BOOK FOR?

There is an old saying in the law business—the man who represents himself has a fool for a client. Yet this book wasn't written for fools, or for you to make a fool of yourself. There are many good reasons why you'd want to represent yourself, and other reasons why you might appreciate the information in this book. Besides, the decision on representation is yours—not the government's, not the bar association's, and not ours.

As we will discuss more in Chapter 6, the United States Constitution guarantees you a lawyer in most criminal proceedings—free if you can't afford one. Yet, people walk into courtrooms every day as criminal defendants and insist on not being represented by a lawyer, though they could have one free.

Many people simply don't like lawyers, don't trust them, and don't want to do business with them. However, they are forced to do business with them when they have legal difficulties. If those difficulties are criminal, these people (now called "defendants") may elect to represent themselves. They are an audience for this book.

You may not dislike lawyers but still do not want one to represent you. You may honestly think that you can do a better job. You, too, are part of the audience for this book.

Some people prefer to represent themselves because they wish to use the criminal proceedings to advance a particular cause or special political concern. Acting on their own behalf is the best way to attract news headlines and attention; acting through a "mouthpiece" doesn't have the same effect. These people may want to use a lawyer in an auxiliary capacity, or fly completely solo. In either case, they can use the information in this book.

Some people can't afford a lawyer. Although they are theoretically available free, they may not be available, or not available free. The public defender system in many states is overwhelmed. Citizens charged with a crime can't expect their public defender to pay the time and attention to their case that it warrants, so they opt to do it themselves. We live in an era of perpetual government budget crises; little by little these affect government services for the poor. There is no reason to think that legal services will be exempt from this problem.

Maybe you have a lawyer, whom you like and wish to handle your case. Still, you'd like to know what is being done every step of the way. For reasons of time, money, or personality, he or she doesn't seem to communicate with you. This book will help you both. It will explain to you what is going on in the courtroom, and prevent you from bothering your lawyer with a lot of worthless (to him or her!) questions.

Perhaps you have a friend or a relative in trouble with the law and you can't find out what's happening in his or her case. This person may be in jail or otherwise unavailable. Maybe neither he or she nor his or her lawyer wants to communicate anything to anyone else, for reasons well or ill. You would still like to know what's happening and to what the various proceedings involving him or her amount. This book is for you as well.

WHAT THIS BOOK COVERS

This book covers the process of fighting a criminal charge in the courtroom. It begins with the questioning or arrest of a suspect, and ends with winning (or losing) the case in a trial.

There are some things that this book addresses, but does not cover in detail. It is not a primer on criminal procedure, though it discusses in some way almost every aspect of criminal trial procedure. Because we are covering many topics in limited space, we have abbreviated or eliminated many details. Nonetheless, we hope what is here, plus the materials in the Appendix, will lead you to other sources for more details if they're necessary.

Nor is this a book on trial tactics. We can't possibly supply all the answers to the questions that come up. We can't give you anything more than some general direction, and maybe a few helpful suggestions. You must use your own judgment, and an enlightened judgment is obviously better than an unenlightened one.

Some chapters in this book, particularly the early ones on confession and searches and seizures, lead off with a small bit of U.S. Constitutional theory. This is a necessary background for later chapters. Much American criminal law is the result of our Constitution. However, this book is not a text for a Constitutional law class. It just has enough to help you understand what's going on and to make intelligent presentations for yourself in the courtroom.

TWO SIMPLE RULES

RULE #1—
USE YOUR
HEAD

In representing and prosecuting persons charged with crimes, I've come to two basic rules that cover every aspect of the criminal law process.

The first rule is to use common sense and think objectively, especially if you defend yourself. If you are a criminal defendant, you can't afford to think emotionally. You don't have professional legal help to think rationally for you. You are just going to have to do it yourself.

We know you are in a tough spot—maybe the toughest of your life. You may be scared or nervous, unable to sleep, eat or get along with anyone else. We've seen this many, many times and we are trying to give you some tips on how to win your case. Winning isn't the main thing. As Vince Lombardi said, it's the only thing.

This rule should also govern the way you dress in court. Other people are judging you and, unfortunately, some people judge others by their appearance. So, if you want to maximize your chances of winning, treat the courtroom not as a fashion contest, but not as a day at the beach either. Dress well but not too well.

This advice on dress also applies to haircuts, nose rings, tattoos, etc.

RULE #2—
BE POLITE

Act politely, even deferentially. Keep quiet unless it's your turn to speak, in which case you say what you have to say. Then sit down and keep quiet again.

Don't make faces or roll your eyeballs when the momentum of the case seems to swing against you. Don't resort to any other cheap tricks—especially if there are jurors around to detect them (and they will). When the judge talks—you listen. You will be given a chance to talk later.

We don't give this advice because of morality, or because it's the nice thing to do, but because it helps you win. You will achieve better results being polite and considerate to the people in court, even the ones who are trying to step on you. This means everybody: your jailers, your judge, your cell mate, your prosecutor, etc.

Language is a mark of politeness. Profanity may have its place, but it rarely belongs in the courtroom.

Another aspect of politeness is keeping your temper. You will find this very difficult to do because there are people in the courtroom who are trying to do hurtful things to you. Still, if you want to get out of this mess, you must keep control of yourself.

Treating people politely is more than just being nice to them. It means treating them with a certain amount of deference. Watch how lawyers in the courtroom act around judges, bailiffs, jailers, etc. They present themselves as if they were presenting themselves to the King. They call them nice names, "Mr.," "Mrs.," "Your Honor," and so on. They smile at them, laugh at their jokes, and sympathize with their woes. I can guarantee you with 100% assurance that they don't act this way because they like these people, or because they are overcome by their high position. When they are outside the courtroom, they will ignore the clerk on the street and bad mouth the judge in the most unspeakable terms. They are oily and polite to them in the courtroom because they want to win. You want to win too, so you should do the same.

If You Are Questioned by The Government

1

The Fifth Amendment

The best advice my mother ever gave me was, "Michael, never miss an opportunity to keep your mouth shut." And that's the best advice I can give you if the government ever questions you about a crime.

Not only is it a good idea to keep your mouth shut, it's your constitutional right to do so. The Fifth Amendment to the United States Constitution says: "No person…shall be compelled in any criminal case to be a witness against himself…." You can't be a witness against yourself if you keep your mouth shut.

The reason for the Fifth Amendment illustrates why it is important. It was adopted by the former British colonists less than 200 years after Great Britain had its own version of the Spanish Inquisition. In Britain this was the Star Chamber, and it was a principal tool for religious oppression. The King could call citizens into his court and force them to testify about their activities. Sometimes the mere dread of facing the King's white-wigged judges provoked confessions. Even in those cases where a citizen in the Star Chamber could testify about his side of the story, the King's ministers could still cross-examine him, catch him in contradictions, or generally make a fool of him. In other words, they could resort to the lawyer's usual bag of tricks, all of which might lead the judges to conclude that the witness was guilty. There were no jury trials in the Star Chamber, and none of the usual common law protections. If that didn't work, the King could always resort to torture.

The ex-colonists were too mindful of these abuses of the Star Chamber to allow their new government to continue them. That's why many of their ancestors had come to the New World. And that's why they adopted the Fifth Amendment.

Today most people probably hear of the Fifth Amendment when gangsters, Communists, or (more recently) White House aides, invoke it in front of congressional committees. They testify with the usual amount of sweating, fidgeting, whispering with their lawyers, and so forth. They may look guilty, but they don't have to say anything more than, "Senator, I take the Fifth on that." But to you, the Fifth Amendment can be of far greater help—for the guilty, the innocent, and the inbetween.

GOVERNMENT INVESTIGATORS

First, understand that the Fifth Amendment means that you are under no obligation to help government investigators who are investigating you. If they can't prove a case against you by their own efforts, it's their tough luck. You don't have to furnish them with words from your own mouth to do the job.

The term "government investigators" merits some explaining. It can mean all sorts of officials—many more than the local police departments and sheriff's deputies you probably think of. These are city or county (parishes in Louisiana) investigators. State governments also have investigators—for instance, the highway patrol. Most states have special criminal investigative bodies to investigate suspected special crimes; they usually refer to these agencies as a State Bureau of Criminal Apprehension, or something similar. At the federal level, there are the famous "alphabet" agencies: the FBI (Federal Bureau of Investigation), CIA (Central Intelligence Agency), DEA (Drug Enforcement

Administration), BATF (Bureau of Alcohol, Tobacco & Firearms), IRS (Internal Revenue Service) and many lesser-known agencies.

The higher you climb the government pyramid, the more specialized and better trained the investigators. That usually means you are in more trouble if you find yourself dealing with them. The Fifth Amendment protects you against all of them. They're on their own. You don't need to help them, and it usually won't be in your best interest to do so.

That's not the end of the list. Administrative agencies at all levels have employees whose job is to question citizens and bring criminal or civil charges against them. The problem with these folks is that they just assume that the citizenry will be happy to deal with them. They're usually interested in some arcane subject like truck weights or welfare checks. They don't look, dress, act, or talk like regular cops. Whatever they call themselves, their line is pretty much the old standard, "I'm from the Government, and I'm here to help you."

Even trickier are government "informants." These can be a fellow worker, a friend, or even a relative, who has turned "stool pigeon"—probably to save his or her own neck and maybe to make a buck by turning on you. Because of other laws that were forming even before the time of the Star Chamber, you probably don't have anything to worry about from your spouse (presuming your marriage is valid in the first place) because of the "spousal privilege" which means a spouse cannot be forced to testify against his or her spouse. This protection doesn't necessarily extend to your children, your parents, or other relatives and friends. The infamous spies, Julius and Ethel Rosenberg, went to the gas chamber because Ethel's brother gave testimony in order to save himself.

WHAT IF I DON'T TALK?

"Can they make it rough on me?" Well, maybe, but probably not as rough as a lengthy stay in prison.

"Will they go easy on me if I cooperate?" Don't ever bet on it. What they really want is what everybody wants—a promotion, a handshake from the boss, a week at the beach. If you confess and make it easy for them to prove the case against you, that investigator will get a host of good things—certainly the esteem of fellow workers, and probably a compliment from the captain on being such a clever interrogator. Maybe they'll promote him or her, and he or she can pay for that trip to Florida with the raise that comes with that promotion. Remember, this is his or her job. He or she goes to work in the morning for the same reasons you do.

A full confession makes everybody else's job easier—everything is real tidy and there's less paperwork to bother with. The police can explain to the victim, "We got the guy." The DA (district attorney), also known as the state's attorney or prosecuting attorney, will just love a ready-made case handed to him or her on a silver platter. The judge won't have to worry about sending someone to prison who maintains he or she is innocent. Yes, it helps everyone else—everyone except you.

"Will they torture me?" Probably not, although in some parts of the country these days I'm not so sure. Again, use your head, and look on the bright side: if they leave bruises you're sure to get that confession tossed out of court.

"Don't they have to keep the promises they made to me?" Not unless it's in writing.

"If I let it all spill out, I'll feel better." Maybe you will. Police prey on the human instinct to win the approval of others by confessing one's sins. Check out the magazine rack at the supermarket; everybody's doing it. Getting the worries of the world off your shoulders may buy you some temporary emotional relief, but it will also buy you a whole lot more trouble.

Be careful. It does you no good to answer "I don't remember" or "I don't recall," if you really do remember. "I don't recall" is an answer in itself, and may have unwanted consequences. You'll not only look foolish if you get a sudden return of memory, but it may be a separate criminal offense if your lack of memory is seen as an effort to deceive or mislead government investigators. The correct answer is " I don't want to talk about it" or "I stand on my right to keep quiet," not "I don't remember."

Part of the training every investigator gets is a thorough schooling in how to interrogate suspects. Plead with them, trick them, bully them, appeal to their sense of justice or basic morality, appeal to their religious beliefs, mention their families (perhaps in a menacing fashion, perhaps in a shameful one), etc. The techniques are not much different from what you might use to get a small child to go to bed. They are household words down at the station house: the "Mutt & Jeff" or "good cop/bad cop" routine, the rubber hose, etc.

YOUR MIRANDA RIGHTS

Whoever, whatever, and however the government chooses to investigate, the important thing to keep in mind is that you don't have to cooperate. Sometimes, the government has the obligation to tell you that you don't have to cooperate. Once people hear that much from the government investigator himself, they're less likely to harm themselves.

This warning originates in the now-famous Miranda rule announced by the U.S. Supreme Court 30 years ago, when individuals' rights seemed just as important as the government's. Today, those warnings are most often seen on television as police officers read rights off a card to a suspect they are arresting.

You may have heard stories about criminals "getting off" because the police didn't read them their rights, or didn't read them properly. This rarely happens. It is more likely that statements or confessions violating Miranda will be inadmissible as evidence at trial. In other words, just because it tricked or squeezed a confession out of you, doesn't mean that the government has to drop the charges against you—not if it has some other evidence against you that it can use in court.

Don't gamble that some judge (who's frequently an ex-prosecutor) will rule later in your favor. That's because the Miranda ruling only applies to a few situations. For instance, it rarely applies to routine traffic stops. Furthermore, the police these days are smart enough to know what those situations are, so they will usually read the rights. Keep in mind that the Fifth Amendment protects you in many circumstances, not just in Miranda situations when the government has to tell you about your rights.

Am I "In Custody"?

The key to deciding when the government has to read you your rights turns on whether you are "in custody." There are some easy examples. You are not in custody when the local sales tax collector stops by your store to see if you are charging the tax. You are free to come and go as you choose. You don't have to cooperate with him or her no matter what he or she tells you or threatens. You are not "in custody." (That doesn't mean there may not be consequences. Your sales tax license may be in jeopardy but you still don't have to say anything.)

At the other end of the spectrum the jail house doors have just clanged shut behind you. You're dressed in prison garb. You may be handcuffed. You are most certainly "in custody" now, and the government must advise you of your rights if it's going to question you about your supposed misdeeds.

For more illustration about what it means to be "in custody" see the next chapter.

DOCUMENT INSPECTIONS; GRAND JURY SUBPOENAS

There are a couple of special situations that implicate your Fifth Amendment rights. First, beware of "documents only" investigations by the government. In other words, the investigator doesn't want to talk to you, he or she only wants to look at your records. Whether he or she can do that (force you to turn them over) is not governed by the Fifth Amendment, but by the Fourth Amendment (see Chapter 3). Remember, what you write or say can and will be used against you in a court of law. A man's best friend may not be his dog, but his fireplace.

Another exception to the Fifth Amendment occurs when the government subpoenas you to testify (usually in front of a Grand Jury). If it gives you immunity from prosecution, it can force you to rattle on about your own misdeeds. This is the way the government gets around the Fifth Amendment. But it pays a price: By immunizing you, it can't prosecute you based on what you say. Confess to the Lindbergh kidnaping or the Oklahoma City bombing. They can't lay a finger on you.

If You Are Arrested or Charged with a Crime

2

Being Arrested

The popular "television" impression of how criminal cases begin is with the arrest. The defendant, sometimes caught red-handed, is placed under arrest by Officer O'Hara, who announces quite simply, "You're under arrest." As we'll discuss here, television is not necessarily reality. Sometimes it's hard to tell if you are "under arrest."

Of course, many arrests do occur that way. The word "arrest" means that the suspect or arrestee is deprived of his or her liberty. The suspect has to go where the arresting officer decides he or she is to go, not where he or she chooses to go.

It's often important for a criminal defendant, or a potential criminal defendant, to find out if he or she is "under arrest," or not. The easiest way to do this is to ask the arresting officer the simple question, "Am I under arrest?" Use some judgment here. Ask the question politely. The officer may respond, "You weren't until now," which obviously doesn't help matters any. Still, it's a wiser move to ask the question than to go on in ignorance.

Unless you find out if you're under arrest, you can't figure out if you can come and go as you please. You can't decide if you have to abide by the instructions of the police. It may be important to find out if you are "in custody" (which you are, if you're under arrest)—to learn if the police have to advise you of your Miranda rights (see the previous chapter on Fifth Amendment rights). So, again with the usual caveat: Don't be afraid to ask.

WHO HAS THE POWER TO ARREST?

With one important qualification (discussed below), the power to arrest doesn't rest with just anyone. In most states, only someone recognized as a "peace officer," or having some similar classification, can make an arrest. This peace officer will be specially trained and certified to obtain "peace officer" status. He or she will probably be a local police officer or a deputy sheriff, though he or she could be a member of some other investigative agency.

The peace officer has powers besides the power to make arrests. In most jurisdictions, only peace officers can wear special uniforms or use other law enforcement identification. In some states peace officers have the authority to carry concealed weapons, to use flashing lights on their vehicles, etc.

Often state investigators, or even the FBI, will not make an arrest on their own. They'll take along a local police officer to actually make the arrest. Maybe they haven't met the local certification required of a peace officer. Maybe they want someone in uniform, obviously armed, who does it all the time.

THE HAZARDS OF ARREST

Since, in making an arrest, the peace officer deprives someone of his or her liberty, he or she has to proceed cautiously but powerfully. This can be a delicate matter, for which the best police forces are thoroughly trained. It is fraught with dangers for both the arrestee and the arresting officer.

The peace officer making an arrest has to have enough power to restrain the suspect. He or she needs to have the willingness to use a gun, billy club, or some other instrument to do what he or she has to do. But the peace officer can't use too much force—not unless he or she wants to deal with a whole host of unwanted and unneeded consequences. He could be exposing himself to a later civil suit for "false arrest" or "police brutality." Internal police investigations, press inquiries, and other unpleasantries could follow.

The suspect in these situations obviously could get hurt, or worse. He or she also runs the risk of committing the crime of "resisting arrest," which is a charge additional to the crime for which he or she is already being arrested. You might want to consult the infamous Rodney King videotape to see if you can figure out at what point the officers crossed the line between a lawful and an unlawful arrest, if they did at all. Two juries disagreed.

THE SUMMONS PROCEDURE

It's not always necessary to begin a criminal charge with an arrest, although many are. Many smaller cases begin with a notice, officially called a summons. The summons simply means that the government requires the defendant to show up in court on a specified day to answer criminal charges brought against him or her.

Just because a summons issues, the defendant will not necessarily be arrested or held in jail if he or she shows up in court. He or she could be, but just by showing up he or she shows that an arrest isn't needed. He or she will probably be allowed to just show up for further court appearances.

On the other hand, if he chooses to disregard the summons, it's almost certain an "arrest warrant" will issue when his or her absence is discovered. The arrest warrant is an order from a local judge, directing some kind of peace officer to find the defendant, arrest him or her, and bring him or her into court to answer the charges. In a sense, the summons is a kind of request, while the arrest warrant is a command.

A routine traffic ticket is probably a summons in your jurisdiction. These are criminal charges because they carry the threat of a fine, or even a jail sentence. Even a parking citation can fit the definition. But unless the officer actually arrests the driver when he or she is stopped for the violation, a traffic ticket is nothing more than a summons. Sometimes the term is a "tab charge." It is simply a notice to show up in traffic court on the day stated. Often no one expects the driver to show. He or she is just expected to mail in the fine. If he or she does nothing (a common occurrence in many traffic courts these days), the offense "goes to warrant." That is, an arrest warrant issues and the traffic police officer will undoubtedly execute it the next time the unlucky driver commits a violation.

THE CITIZEN'S ARREST

One exception to the requirement that a police or peace officer make the actual arrest is the "citizen's arrest." Despite the occasional news story when it does happen, it's exceedingly rare for the "man on the street" to make an arrest out of the clear blue sky.

Most citizen's arrests are made by security personnel or store clerks. These people are not certified peace officers, although they can be (that's why many businesses hire off-duty police for part-time work). They are guards, detectives, private patrols, and store owners or shopkeepers. Usually, local law gives these persons a recognized but limited license to detain offenders.

The citizen's arrest has a long history—back to the common law. Then it was not only a right for private citizens to make an arrest; in some circumstances that right could be an obligation. The citizen's arrest may be more important in the future if the rate of lawbreaking, and the limitations on size of police departments, continue.

The law recognizes and protects the citizen's arrest to insure the person making the arrest isn't financially liable for a false arrest or for personal injury. If he or she is depriving someone else of liberty, he or she could be committing a crime unless there's some justification in the law. As with a routine police officer arrest, perhaps even more so, the whole situation is clearly rife with the danger of personal injury.

There is great variation in the United States of the authority of citizens to make their own arrest. Most states follow the common law distinction between misdemeanors and felonies. You could not make an arrest for a misdemeanor unless it's committed in your presence, but you could make an arrest for any felony with probable cause.

You are most likely to find yourself in a citizen's arrest when a shopkeeper detains you for suspected shoplifting. In most states he or she has to notify the police immediately that he or she has done this, and they will send out an officer to finish things up. Another common situation occurs in barroom brawls. Someone, perhaps even the opposing assailant, sits on the prospective arrestee until the police can arrive.

In a sense, citizen's arrests are instances of "might makes right." There will not be any kind of an arrest unless the one citizen possesses the temporary power to detain the other. If the arrest is a valid one, and the suspect chooses to force his or her way past the shopkeeper, he or she could be criminally liable for resisting arrest if he or she is caught later. If it's not a valid arrest, it's the shopkeeper who has trouble. (More commonly, the suspect belts the shopkeeper and runs past him or her to freedom. Now there's been an assault, and maybe resisting arrest, but not an arrest.)

Being "Under Arrest"

There's a popular misconception that an arrested person is entitled to "one phone call." Most people presume the police have to let them make one telephone call to anyone they choose when they're placed under arrest. This is legend. There is no constitutional requirement that the police must allow you to make this call. State statutes rarely guarantee any such phone call. The police don't have to let you communicate with anyone when you're under arrest except an attorney, and for that they have to let you communicate more than once, if necessary.

As a matter of common decency and good public relations, though, and to maintain some order within, most jails will allow inmates contact by telephone with just about anyone. They'll also allow most inmates non-attorney visitors. They may restrict the hours, and your visitor will need to be sober. There may also be limits on dealings which might make up further criminal activity.

This is not a book designed to help you deal with the very unpleasant status of being incarcerated. All I can suggest is that you try to use the common sense and common courtesy we talked about in the Introduction of this book. Those things will help.

Still, this book does try to help you defend yourself against criminal charges, and there are several things that do happen in "the joint" that have a direct impact on that. First, do not assume that your fellow-inmates are necessarily "soul brothers" who view the case against you to be the trumped-up basket of lies that you know it to be. They may be looking for a way to help their own defense, and a good way to do that is to turn on someone else. They will be happy to appear as a witness in your case and testify that you confessed everything to them while in jail. They may do this whether it happens or not; jailhouse informants have a poor record for reliability. It is suggested that you not talk to anyone about the charges against you. In fact, don't trust your co-inmates for much of anything. Friendship with them will do little to help you win.

Second, accepting any kind of contraband or getting into any kind of fight is a bad idea.

Also, don't get too familiar with the jailhouse staff. I don't understand why that happens from either end. It doesn't do any defendant much good in the courtroom.

If the Police Raid Your Home, Car or Business 3

Reasonable Searches and Seizures; Probable Cause

The specific provision of the U.S. Constitution that governs "searches and seizures" is the Fourth Amendment to the Constitution. That amendment reads:

> *The right of the people to be secure in their persons, houses, papers, and effects, against unreasonable searches and seizures, shall not be violated, and no Warrants shall issue, but upon probable cause, supported by Oath or affirmation, and particularly describing the place to be searched, and the persons or things to be seized.*

This is a complicated amendment. Note that it requires two separate things: First, it restricts the government (meaning the police) to conduct only "reasonable" searches and seizures. Second, it requires that whoever issues warrants have something called "probable cause."

Ideally, if the world worked strictly by the book, only very unusual searches and seizures would be done without a warrant—during an arrest or a chase, for example. In the usual situation, the police would have ample time and means to present their reasons for requesting a warrant to a magistrate (judge, justice of the peace, etc.). The magistrate could then decide if there was probable cause to justify the search. He she would then issue the warrant, and the search would meet the requirement that it be "reasonable."

But the world doesn't work by the book. Searches and seizures arise in the world of law enforcement, and in that world many other considerations and factors are at work. Over the years, the courts, particularly the United States Supreme Court, have spent much time fashioning rules and policies that apply the 54 words in the text of the Fourth Amendment to the real life world.

Let's begin by detailing the kinds of searches that you might find yourself involved in.

SOME COMMON SEARCH SITUATIONS

Imagine yourself, or maybe somebody you know, walking along a dimly lit and isolated city street just outside the central business district. It's early in the morning after all the taverns and stores have closed. A squad car drives by and shines its search light on you. It then wheels about and pulls up next to you. An officer leaves his car and asks what you're doing. Let's assume he doesn't receive an acceptable answer. He tells you to turn around and face the wall, and starts to frisk you. Can he get away with this?

Or, suppose you are driving your own automobile, but not in your home state. You have a passenger with you who is very definitely of Hispanic origin: he looks like Fidel Castro and speaks only Spanish. You're pulled over for a routine traffic check. Maybe you had a tail light out. The police officer spots your passenger and asks enough questions to realize he's probably dealing with a foreign national. He demands to look in the trunk of your car. Can he do that? Does he need a warrant?

Or suppose a police officer arrives on the front steps of your home and announces that he wants to look around the place a little. He's especially interested in your bedroom closet. "You wouldn't mind now, sir, would you?" How should you answer?

Another scenario: You're quietly minding the books of your business when an agent of a federal, state, or local taxing authority enters. He demands to see those books and accounts—pronto. Do you have to turn them over? Right now?

Change this scenario a little. Imagine it's not an agent of the taxing authority, but an agent of the state administrative bureau that licenses and regulates your particular kind of business. Do you have to share your records with him or her? Does it make any difference if he or she has a warrant?

Be patient. These questions will soon be answered.

General Principles

There are hundreds of variations on these basic scenarios. Each describes a search, or the lead-in to a search, by the government of a citizen or his or her property. Each could amount to nothing, or could become the basis for major criminal charges against the citizen.

In answering the questions posed by these scenarios, it is important to have a few clear principles in mind about searches and seizures. Often you can't consult a lawyer, because you can't find one, or you can't explain the complications of the situation to him or her then and there. You are going to have to make up your own mind what to do.

What is a search and seizure? A "search" occurs whenever an agent of the government makes an inspection or review of something that you ordinarily think of as private. It could be on your person, in your car, or in some place that you don't ordinarily have spectators (a telephone conversation, for example). If that same agent gathers evidence from the search, for use later in criminal proceedings, it's a "seizure." There are many exceptions and qualifications to the rules governing searches and seizures, but the law is pretty clear that the scenarios we've posed here are searches, and involve potential seizures.

As a rule, no search can proceed without some kind of reason. If the reason is above the level of mere suspicion, then it's probably good enough to qualify as probable cause (what the police call "PC"). The officer cannot stop and search anyone, anytime he or she feels like it. The officer can ask to search, but without a reason he or she can't forcibly insist on it. A judge will later decide if the reason is any good. If he or she decides to, and has the time and opportunity to, check it out with the magistrate first, then he or she is applying for a search warrant. Again, he or she has to have some kind of reason, and as the Fourth Amendment says, that reason has to amount to "probable cause."

It's useful to understand how the cases in which the courts decide these general principles arise. Typically the police will do the search and seize the evidence, and later try to use it in court to convict someone of a crime. First, the trial court, and then perhaps an appellate court, will decide if the evidence was seized constitutionally, in a sort of watchdog role after the fact.

THE "STOP AND FRISK"

Let's return to our scenario where the police stopped you on that dimly-lit, deserted downtown street early in the morning. This scenario happens hundreds of times every day. It's known as a "stop and frisk." It still technically falls within the category of a search. The courts (in deference to the danger the situation poses to all concerned) have generally held that it is not unreasonable for the police to conduct a preliminary pat-down or check of the suspect. The reason for that is to be sure the suspect doesn't have a gun or other dangerous weapon.

Police officers obviously have to have a certain amount of safety to do their job at all. So it is just about impossible to later object to a stop and frisk because it didn't constitute a reasonable search or seizure. Problems usually arise with the "stop and frisk" because of something else. The possibility of finding a weapon justifies the search, but if no weapon is found, but something else is found (for example, narcotics), it won't be held inadmissible later in court. In other words, the police had a reasonable basis to search for one kind of evidence. They didn't find it. They found something else, yet that something else is not something they had probable cause to search for in the first place. Such a search is constitutional. If evidence is found during the pat-down, it can be used later against the suspect.

So it's almost impossible to have the results of a stop and frisk thrown out as evidence in the courtroom. As we'll dwell on in later chapters, the police can be clever in creating explanations of the danger they seem to find themselves in. So they will steer the description of the stop or search into the category of the stop and frisk. So, the short answer to the first question we asked in this chapter is: "Yes, they can get away with it."

There's more to it than that. Any suspect who tries to assert his or her rights or tries to physically resist the pat down is in for a rough time. The police will read this attitude as an indication that he or she really has something to hide. They will cuff the suspect or bring him or her to the ground upon the slightest hint of a lack of cooperation, and later charge him or her with resisting arrest. Even if they're wrong, even if the suspect had nothing to hide, the courts will usually back up the police. In other words, you can be 100% innocent of anything, but get rough handling from the police and a charge of resisting arrest, just by being on that dark, dimly-lit street early in the morning.

THE CAR SEARCH

Rarely is there much danger of the car, or something in its trunk, being used as a weapon against the police. So the rationale of police safety won't justify any exception to the constitutional rule that the police need a reason to search the trunk. Still, most car searches pass constitutional muster, but on different reasoning.

Automobiles are mobile. The police know that if they don't search that trunk now, there's a very good (like 100%) chance that when they come back with a warrant, the illegal contraband in the trunk or the car itself won't be there. So police have a good deal of latitude in impounding the vehicle and searching its contents—including the trunk.

How far can that search go? Can the police look under the seats, pull out seats, open the glove compartment, rip open the frame? Let's assume they have enough probable cause to impound the car. That means that the car goes with the police, not with you, back to wherever they want to conduct the search in their own sweet time. Its driver and occupants are detained.

Because it's not an emergency, any search has to be made under a warrant based on probable cause, just as if it were a non-emergency search of someone's home. The police have to have a reason, and have to write out that reason in a search warrant application. A local magistrate reviews this application. The officer applying for the warrant takes an oath before the magistrate when he or she presents the warrant. It is the magistrate, not the police, who decides whether there's to be a search at all.

That description sounds like all the i's will be dotted, and all the t's crossed when the police present their application to the magistrate. On paper, they are. In the real world, however, search warrant applications are anything but neat and tidy. Often they are assembled in a hurry. They are shown to the magistrate at odd hours, such as right after lunch, just before he or she leaves for home, etc. He or she signs off without thinking much about them.

The magistrate is probably a local judge and doesn't have a lot of time to read through search warrants. After all, he or she considers himself or herself a big shot. The police paperwork is given a quick glance, and the officer a perfunctory oath. He or she asks the officer: "You read this stuff? Is it all true?" The magistrate signs the search warrant and returns to his or her "more important" tasks.

Of course, there are careful, studious judges who read every application and carefully balance whether the officer has "probable cause" for the search, or just a "mere suspicion." Those judges exist. There are also judges who are nothing more than political hacks and have little regard for the Constitution or for the sanctity of your car trunk.

THE CONSENT SEARCH

Earlier we posed a scenario in which the police officer asked if he or she could search your home, focusing on that bedroom closet. If you answered the question, "Yes" (whether you really mean it or not), the courts will later hold that you have consented to the search. You can't complain later if he or she finds anything.

If you answered, "No way. Yeah, I do mind. Get out of here," you are fully within your Fourth Amendment rights. Of course, he she will take note of your answer and your attitude. If the officer has nothing more than suspicions, he or she will bide his or her time. He or she may watch your home, from every angle, day and night (which may be noticed by your neighbors).

The police will little by little gather scraps of suspicion that they'll build into probable cause for their search warrant application. When they think their suspicions rise to the level of probable cause, they'll head back downtown to ask that local magistrate for that warrant. Count on seeing the police again.

Many homeowners, and most drivers, faced with a request for a consensual car search, will simply consent to the search. They'll hope the police can't find anything incriminating, or won't find anything they can't explain. They take their chances, figuring a consent to a search might at least allay some suspicions.

That may not be your smartest tactic if your car or home is hiding contraband. It's probably better to require the officers to secure a warrant or otherwise show probable cause for that search warrant. Yes, you will be under greater suspicion. Yes, your neighbors will wonder what's going on over there. But if you are ever to contest the reasonableness of the search, or the probable cause for the warrant, you can't consent to the search.

Remember, that warrant is looked at a second time and maybe a third. The second time is during or before trial, when both sides are present to argue about whether there was probable cause for the search. If the judge rules there was probable cause, he or she has to be convincing enough for his or her colleagues on the appeals court, where the warrant will get a third review. It's a whole different world in the appeals court.

What to Do During a Search

If the police do conduct a search of your home and you are present in the home at the time, ask to leave. You don't want to try to leave without asking, just in case the police consider you to be under arrest. Remember, the easiest way to find out if you are under arrest is to ask whoever is in charge of the search: "Am I under arrest?" If he or she says you are not, your next comment is, "Fine, I'm leaving." Some police don't understand that much. If they force you to stay, they've effectively put you under arrest, and they had better have grounds to do so.

The reason you should leave is to make it impossible for you to give the police any help during the search. The police are going to give you many reasons why you shouldn't leave, even if they recognize you are within your rights by doing so. They will tell you that they will leave the place wide open, that they can't be responsible for what happens, etc. That's fine. Those are all phony reasons. They want you there to make their job easier. You know your own house pretty well and can probably lead them directly to whatever they want to see. If they get near contraband, you'll no doubt be nervous. If you start talking to them, you'll only give away information.

Just leave. If you're not there, you can't say anything to the police, or give something away by a guilty look or a knowing glance. You are under no obligation to help the police out in this search. You don't have to point things out or move furniture. They can make things difficult by opening up crates, boxes, etc., but that's the price you pay for exercising your constitutional right not to help them. The police have a certain amount of authority to be destructive of your personal property if they must do so to search for evidence. Let them be destructive. You can always replace that stuff anyway.

If you stay, should you try to hide anything? Absolutely not—unless you can get away with it, and you probably can't. If you stay, the police will pay as much attention to you as they will to your home and its belongings.

OTHER WARRANTLESS SEARCHES

HOT PURSUIT

Another circumstance in which the courts have held that the police don't need a warrant to conduct a search is the "hot pursuit." This occurs when the police chase a suspect who is attempting to evade their grasp. The circumstance by itself provides enough probable cause.

INCIDENT TO AN ARREST

Another common warrantless search is "incident to an arrest." Here, the search occurs at the same time the police arrest the suspect. If the arrest is lawful (that is, if it is warranted by probable cause), it's not unreasonable for the police to search the suspect. This is similar to the stop-and-frisk search, except that the suspect is placed under arrest first. Such a search can extend beyond the suspect's person. It can, and usually does, include any of his or her personal effects that are transportable, and his or her automobile (if he or she is arrested in or near it). It may include the area of the arrest—even an entire home or business.

IN OFFICER'S
PRESENCE

Another common warrantless search, in which the courts routinely support the police decision to search, occurs where an offense has been or is being committed in the police officer's presence. The police don't have to actually make the arrest. They may have enough justification to conduct the search without the arrest. If they find something, of course, the arrest will follow.

CONSEQUENCES

If a judge later rules that the police search of your home, car, or business violates the Fourth Amendment, what happens then? The only direct consequence of this constitutional violation is that any evidence gathered against you because of the search will be "suppressed." That is, it will not be received as evidence against you in any trial, though it might be valid evidence in certain non-trial proceedings. If the trial court admitted the evidence, and the jury convicted you at trial, but the appeals court later rules the search was unconstitutional, your conviction will be reversed (probably) and you will get a new trial.

That may or may not make a big difference—sometimes the evidence improperly gathered is not important and the prosecution can proceed anyway. But sometimes there simply can be no case against you without that evidence. For example, if you are charged with possession of narcotics, the government won't get very far without having those narcotics as evidence. In such cases the prosecutor often dismisses the case.

There can be other consequences to an improper police raid. You may recover money damages from the government body for this deprivation of your civil rights. This subject is governed by civil law rather than criminal law, and there is a host of qualifications and restrictions on such lawsuits. You might be forced to sue the individual police officers involved in the raid; in many areas, where the local police are looked upon as local heroes, you will not come into court from the best position.

PROPERTY FORFEITURES

In recent years, the war on drugs has generated a unique kind of government seizure of personal property known as the "forfeiture." Government agents have always seized contraband when they found it. They routinely take and keep property which citizens have no right to possess, usually drugs, pornography, illegal cigarettes or guns, or alcohol during the Prohibition era.

Such property became evidence at trial. Since it was illegal to own it in the first place, the court wouldn't return it to the citizen at the end of trial. The government kept it and usually just destroyed it. (In some famous cases, illegal narcotics somehow found their way back out onto the street even after being in the police department evidence room.)

But since about the mid-1980s the government has been seizing property that is perfectly legal to possess—money, cars, houses, even land. These seizures, known as "forfeitures," are done because the property was somehow used to commit a crime, probably a drug crime. The clearest and probably most frequent example of this is using an automobile to sell narcotics. Not only are the narcotics seized, and used as evidence at trial, but the automobile is seized as well. The owner "forfeits" his or her rights to it in favor of the government, which then probably sells it off at auction. It may not matter who owns the auto. The arrested person may not be the owner. The theory is that the owner has the responsibility to see to it that his property is only legally used.

There have been some real stretches of logic to justify these forfeitures. There have been instances in which entire farms have been seized because marijuana was growing on some small parcel. The marijuana grower may not have been the owner of the farm, but only a tenant farmer or a relative of the farmer. If the government is authorized to grab that property by forfeit, the farm owner is simply out of luck.

The government may have no intention of using this property as evidence at any trial; it only intends for you not to keep it. It's sold off to someone else, with the government pocketing the proceeds.

Not only does this seem unfair at first glance, the laws authorizing property forfeitures often build in a profit motive for the government agency doing the seizing. Sometimes, the money from the sale of forfeited property goes directly back to the law enforcement agency that seized it in the first place. In other words, the local police get to use the proceeds from the sale of your car to pay their own salaries, or maybe just fix up the station house. The legislature has empowered the bureaucracy to feed itself by grabbing property it claims citizens are using to commit crimes.

If that's not bad enough, the procedures set up for the citizen to fight a forfeiture are cumbersome and expensive. Immediately upon seizing your property, the government will probably drop a civil complaint on you to complete the forfeiture of your property. You must respond to that complaint within a matter of days. If you fail to do so, your property is irretrievably lost.

The subject of contesting property forfeitures is beyond the subject matter of this book. But it is important for someone who is fighting a criminal case to understand that when his or her property is seized, he or she is not necessarily going to get it back. It may not even make any difference that he or she is ultimately found "not guilty" of the crime charged. He or she must act immediately to contest the forfeiture. Waiting until after the criminal case is over is tantamount to giving up.

How Criminal Cases Get Started **4**

Who Prosecutes

No matter how it begins, by peace officer arrest, by citizen's arrest, or by summons, at some point any criminal case will go through the offices of a prosecuting authority. That's the only way the government can bring criminal charges against you. The prosecutor is the government official (almost always a lawyer) who presents the criminal charges to the court. If you are the defendant, the prosecutor is as much your enemy as the police.

In the United States, there is a vast and powerful bureaucracy of prosecutors that more-or-less corresponds to the bureaucracy of police and government investigators. In other words, for local crimes investigated by the local police, there will be a city prosecutor. At the county level, corresponding to the sheriff's office, there will be an official probably known as the District Attorney (or County Attorney, Prosecuting Attorney, State's Attorney, etc.). This is usually the principal office of general state prosecution authority. Although they have other duties, State Attorneys' General have some authority to prosecute crimes. On the Federal level, complementing the system of the FBI, DEA, etc., are the United States Attorneys. These are found in every state and federal territory, and all are under the general authority of the U.S. Attorney General.

Despite the complexity of this system, each prosecutor's office has a common structure. The chief officer, the one who actually has the title "District Attorney" or "United States Attorney" in a given area, will be a political or quasi-political official. He or she may be elected, or appointed by some political body. Often, he or she will act and react as you expect a politician to act and react. He or she will be helped by a coterie of Assistant D.A.s or Assistant U.S. Attorneys, who of course will do all the "real work" on any case.

Keep some things in mind in dealing with these offices, which are like most law offices. The assistants, those "worker bees," may be young. If they've been on board for a couple of years, though, they no doubt resent the fact that they do all the work. They also resent the fact that the boss does little but deal with the press or other politicians. They're no doubt angling for his or her job.

The DA and his or her staff will have a support staff of secretaries, paralegals, auditors, investigators, etc., who will handle the paperwork presented by the case. These folks will arrange for witnesses, interface with the police or other investigators, etc. No matter what they call themselves, nor how many of them there are, many will be young (the jobs don't often pay that well). You can be sure that all view themselves as very badly overworked and underpaid—and often, they'll be right.

Although the criminal defendant only sees such of these people that come into the courtroom, they are definitely out there and have much power over the course of his or her case. The defendant is outnumbered. His or her knowledge of the tensions that exist in the prosecution office is one of the few advantages he or she has.

THE COMPLAINT OR INDICTMENT

The charges against you will be written out in a document called the "complaint." If there have been grand jury proceedings, the charges will be written out in a similar document known as an "indictment."

You have a right to a copy of this complaint or indictment. Even though it may not make much sense to you, and may be embarrassing to hear read aloud, you can insist that the judge read it to you at your first appearance. If you don't understand it, the judge will explain it.

At the beginning of the document, as in just about every other paper used in court, will be a heading that identifies the document as one concerning your case. Somewhere in the document there will be a list of the actual charges, and a reference (also known as a "citation") to the particular law of your state (or federal law) that the prosecution claims you violated. Often there will also be a section that describes what the prosecution claims you did in greater detail, no doubt laying out names, dates, places, etc. This is the "list of particulars" or "probable cause section." It won't tell you everything, but it should give you a general view of the case against you.

YOUR FIRST COURT APPEARANCE

You will probably come to court to face these charges soon after your arrest or after you receive a summons. This is only the first in a series of court appearances.

There are several purposes to this first appearance, all of which may seem perfunctory. It is designed to make sure that the defendant is present in court. If he or she is under arrest, the judge decides if bail is going to be granted. The first appearance will decide if the defendant will have an attorney represent him or her, and who that will be. The judge might appoint a public defender if the defendant doesn't have a lawyer, but wants one and can't afford one.

At the first appearance, the court will probably set a schedule for later hearings, according to the local rules. Criminal cases usually proceed by a strict timetable to make sure the defendant receives a "speedy" trial (which might not occur for many months). The first appearance will likely schedule those later hearings, or at least the next in the series of hearings.

The first appearance starts the case formally in the court system. The phase of being arrested is really preliminary to any court involvement. If you're arrested, the police will arrange for you to get to that hearing. If you receive a summons, it will list the time and place of the hearing to which you are being summoned to attend.

You won't have to do much at the first appearance. The judge, or perhaps a clerk, will ask you your name and birth date, and will generally advise you of your rights. He or she may read the charges to you, as we mentioned earlier. He or she will ask if you have a lawyer or want a lawyer, and advise you what sort of system your state has to provide a lawyer to the poor. Finally, he or she will set a date for your next court appearance and tell you to be sure to make it. This much is all pretty routine.

BAIL

One function that also will take place at this initial appearance will no doubt be most important to you—whether bail will be set, and whether you will be able to make that bail and get out of jail.

Bail is another idea that dates from the common law. It is simply money deposited with the court, or the promise to pay money or forfeit property to the court, to guarantee that you will come to your next court appearance. Often, especially in smaller cases, no bail is required. The defendant is placed on a status of NBR—"no bail required,"

RPR—"released on personal recognizance," ROR—"released on own recognizance," or he or she makes a PRB—"personal recognizance bond." Whatever it's called, the judge has made a decision to trust the defendant to show up for the next court appearance without having to put down any money.

There is a difference between the terms "bail" and "bond," although many people use them interchangeably. Bail is the amount of money or property required by the court. Bond is a sum of money (usually about 10% of the bail amount) that is the fee charged by a bail bondsman who guarantees the bail to the court.

A popular misconception confuses the payment of bail with the payment of a fine for traffic offenses. When you "pay a ticket," you may not be paying a fine at all, but may just be making a bail deposit which will then be converted to a fine when you are adjudged guilty of the offense. You probably won't be there and may have forgotten all about the matter. Your bail has been used to pay your fine.

When the judge does set bail, you obviously have the opportunity to pay it. You can just pay the money into the court and you will gain your release. If you make all your court appearances, the money will be returned to you at the conclusion of the case. The court system usually assigns the task of handling the cash and the paperwork to a clerk's office.

If you don't have money or property to post as bond, you may be able to use the service of a bail bondsmen. These are independent business-people who, for a fee, put up the full amount of bail for you. This fee (which you don't get back) is typically 10-20% of the total amount of bail. For example, if bail is set by the court at $5,000, you will pay the bondsman $500 to $1,000. Sometimes a bail bondsman will impose an additional requirement that you pledge your house or personal property to secure your appearance. Some states have enacted a 10% requirement, which means you can put up 10% of the bail to effect your release, thereby making bail bondsmen unnecessary in such jurisdictions.

The bail bondsman has joined forces with you, in a sense. He or she has promised to pay the full amount of your bail if you don't make your court appearances. He or she is taking a real risk and would be most unhappy should you fail to show.

The United States Constitution does forbid "excessive" bail, but it does not guarantee a right to bail in all cases. The government can require defendants in some cases to remain in custody until their case has been disposed of, which may be by trial several months away. This usually occurs when there is a risk of the defendant leaving the jurisdiction rather than facing the charges. (It has not been unknown for drug peddlers to have enough cash to pay bail in an amount of several thousands of dollars, but never be seen again.)

In most serious felony cases there will be no bail, or the bail will be so high that no one could possibly pay it. So for all practical purposes it's nonexistent. Sometimes this is due to the character of the defendant, but more often it's due to the nature of the charges.

CONDITIONAL RELEASE

If you do make bail or are released on your own recognizance, your release may be conditional. In other words, besides paying the bail, you will have to do certain other things to stay out of jail while awaiting trial.

The local probation office, "pretrial services," or some similar office set up for this purpose, will supervise your conditional release. The war on drugs (and the consequent use of urinalysis to detect drugs) has led to a sizeable increase in the number and size of these offices.

A supervised release requires you to check in routinely with the supervising office, much like someone on probation checks in with his or her probation officer. This is done to make sure you are still around. As mentioned above, you may have to give a urine sample if sobriety or being drug-free is one condition of your release. There may be other conditions: for example, having no contact with any unsavory types, such as your co-defendants, or with the victim of your offense, or maintaining your employment, or not leaving the jurisdiction.

If you violate any of these conditions, and if the judge thinks the violation is serious enough, it's just like not making your court appearances. Your bail will be revoked, or forfeited if you're not around. A "bench warrant" will issue for your arrest (so called because the judge will issue it right from his bench, without giving you any notice or a chance to reply).

If your bail is forfeited, your bail bondsman will be most displeased. If you are not around, he or she will change sides. He or she will now join forces with the police and come looking for you. Given that your bail bondsman has money on the line, he or she will probably be leading the pack.

Of course, if you are apprehended after jumping bail or violating a condition of your release, your chances of getting bail again are slim, and that's an optimistic assessment.

Understanding the Charges Against You 5

The crime that you are charged with will fall into one or more of the several categories of crimes described in this chapter. Understanding the categories of crimes, and how the law defines crimes is essential to your defense. You will make many strategic and tactical moves in your defense that will rest on these criminal law definitions.

This chapter may seem long and technical, but then a good deal of the criminal law is long and technical. For reasons that may not be obvious right now, the material in this chapter is vitally important to you. If you want to follow our suggestions about finding the sources of American criminal law, the best place to start is at your local law library. You might be surprised how helpful a law librarian will be to someone in your shoes—you obviously need the help, and you're not one of those haughty lawyers who are always demanding help. Don't be afraid to ask.

The Sources of Criminal Law

The basic source of the all criminal law throughout the world is the fundamental moral code, sometimes called "natural law," that exists in every human society. This code crops up in fairly standard fashion in every society (laws against murder or theft, for example). Some elements appear in all societies, but in different forms from one to the other. Laws against family and sex offenses are probably the most common occurrence of laws that appear everywhere, but in different forms.

The source of the definitions of crime in America (except in Louisiana, where French law had greater influence) is the "common law" that developed in medieval England. For over a thousand years, this body of law was unwritten, but known to the King's judges who applied it. This was called the "common law," because it stemmed from the customs and practices of the people in their everyday affairs. The American colonists brought this "common law" from England, and made it the basis of the first laws of the original colonies. It made its way into the United States Constitution, and after that into the laws of all states and American territories.

The "common law" contained definitions of the most widely-recognized criminal offenses: burglary, robbery, murder, rape, etc. These definitions were unwritten at first. The judges were just expected to know them. In many states these common law definitions are the basis of the current definitions of these crimes.

All state governments, and the federal government, have enacted definitions of these standard crimes that differ from the common law. They have also added many new definitions of what is criminal conduct. These modifications of the common law, and new offenses, are "codified" (that is, written down) in the statutes enacted by the state and federal legislatures. Therefore, lawyers and judges often speak of crimes as having a "statutory law" source or a "common law" source. The difference often depends on how much modification the legislative statutes make to the common law definitions.

You may not think that knowing which of the Ten Commandments is the source of the charges against you is very important. You may not think it's important to know whether the offense charges against you stem from "statutory" or "common" law. You are probably right. Nevertheless, these distinctions are the first steps in classifying the offense, and knowing the precise classification of the offense may be crucial in defending yourself against the charge.

FELONIES AND MISDEMEANORS

The common law made a fundamental distinction between "major" crime and "minor" crime. Even in medieval England, major crimes were typically those in which serious damage was done to another's person or property. The common law called these "felonies," which referred to the punishment of forfeiting lands, property, or life to the crown when they were committed.

Today, while forfeiture is sometimes a punishment for crimes, the term felony generally refers to any offense for which the punishment is more than one year in jail. The standard list of felonies in medieval England are still felonies in modern America, with few variations.

Any crimes for which the punishment is a year or less in jail are "misdemeanors," a term that also designated lesser crimes at common law. Many states have created other distinctions or classifications of misdemeanors that further correlate with the amount of punishment that is possible. The higher classifications of these are "high misdemeanors" or "gross misdemeanors," while the lower categories (those with lesser punishments) are "simple misdemeanors" and "petit (or petty) misdemeanors."

Sometimes the same conduct may be a greater or lesser offense depending on when it's committed. For instance, the crime of drunk driving is typically a simple (or ordinary) misdemeanor. If there have been multiple convictions (for example, if a driver has had previous "DWI" convictions within a designated period), that same conduct can be ranked at a higher level under state statutes. It's probably a "high misdemeanor," and a greater fine or jail sentence is possible.

The category of "petit misdemeanors" refers to minor offenses that are still crimes, but can't result in a jail sentence. These are usually of the traffic ticket or disorderly conduct variety, although more serious driving violations (termed "moving offenses") can rise to the "simple misdemeanor" category.

Closely related to the petit misdemeanor is the "ordinance violation." This is an act not forbidden by the common law or by state statute, but forbidden by an ordinance enacted by the local county or city. These offenses are minor, and may only involve the payment of a monetary fine. These are often the offenses for which you might want to defend yourself, rather than hire an attorney.

The distinction between felonies and misdemeanors, and the further classification of misdemeanors, is often a crucial one. Many consequences for conviction of a crime depend on what level the crime falls into. For instance, serving time for a felony generally takes place in a state penitentiary, while time served for misdemeanors generally takes place in county jails or workhouses. You can lose your "civil rights" (which includes the right to vote or bear arms, among other things) upon conviction of a felony, but that isn't a consequence of a misdemeanor violation. Trial of a petit misdemeanor is often only before a local judge or magistrate. The right to a jury trial doesn't take hold unless the charge is more serious than that. Some states grant a traditional 12-person jury trial for felonies, but try misdemeanors by 6-person juries.

Finally, many states have a classification of "capital crimes" for which the penalty can be execution. These are usually murder or treason, and perhaps rape or a few other serious felonies. Some states preserve the term capital crime, although they no longer use capital punishment.

THE DEGREES OF A CRIME

These offenses against the person of another illustrate another classification of criminal conduct in the law: by "degrees." This term refers to a further subclassification of a common law or statutory criminal offense depending on how serious it is. For instance, in most states, "first degree murder" or "murder in the first degree" is a killing of another that is intentional and "premeditated," or planned out in advance. If the killing is intentional but not premeditated, it becomes "second degree murder." "First degree manslaughter" is a killing done "in the heat of passion." "Second degree manslaughter" means a killing done through negligence or by the misuse of a dangerous weapon. Some states may use other terms, such as "murder" and "aggravated murder," in place of second degree murder and first degree murder.

Assaults, and many other offenses, are also sub-classified by their relative seriousness. "First degree assault" usually involves the infliction of serious bodily harm. If the harm is not serious, but involved the use of a weapon, the assault is usually "second degree." Lesser degrees of assault may involve permanent, but not serious, bodily harm. An assault that results in a broken nose is most likely an assault of a greater degree than one that results in a bloody nose. Some states raise the degree of an assault depending on the status of the victim. For instance, an assault on a police officer typically has a more serious penalty than if it is committed upon an ordinary citizen.

The fact that a crime is against a person, or is of one degree or another, usually has no bearing on whether it's a felony or a misdemeanor. For instance, every state has a category of less-serious assault that is a misdemeanor, and one or more categories of more-serious assaults that are felonies. The variations on this pattern are too many to detail here. Included in the Appendix to this book is information on how to find the particular laws of your state for the finer distinctions of these offenses.

PARTICULAR CRIMES

CRIMES
AGAINST THE
PERSON

Most people consider murder as the most serious crime. It makes up one of several acts which, in some sense, violates the body of another person. The most common of these other acts are assaults and manslaughter. At common law, manslaughter referred to the unlawful killing of another, but done without malice or without deliberation. If the killing was done maliciously, and was planned or thought-out in advance ("malice aforethought"), the killing is murder, not manslaughter. This common law distinction carries forward to today: when death occurs due to an accident or carelessness, and not because of any intention to kill, it is manslaughter, not murder. And you might be surprised to learn that you can be guilty of murder when you are not the actual killer. If you're in the act of committing a felony (say, a robbery) and someone is killed during it, whether by your hand or not, or even without your knowledge or over your protests, you could be held guilty for the murder. This is known as the "felony murder" doctrine.

Assault, or as it is sometimes called, "assault and battery," means the unwanted physical attack upon another person that does not result in death. Technically, the threat to do physical harm, for example, just raising one's hand with the intent to strike, is the "assault." The "touching," or follow through, is what is the "battery."

Other crimes against the person may include kidnaping, abduction, and false imprisonment. These involve the restraint or holding of another person against his or her will, for money or otherwise. Also in this group is the crime of coercion, which is forcing another to commit a criminal act; and criminal libel or defamation, which is really a kind of assault upon another person's reputation rather than upon his or her physical person.

PROPERTY CRIMES Offenses against another's property, rather than his or her physical person, form another common category of criminal activity. Many property crimes are as serious as, or more serious than, crimes against the person. For instance, the crime of extortion involves forcing someone to pay money under the threat of physical harm; the penalty for this offense is usually greater than for a misdemeanor assault.

Sometimes the seriousness of a property crime depends on the particular means used to obtain money. The crime of forgery means the false authentication of a check or other document used to transfer money. Obtaining money by forgery is usually a more serious offense than obtaining it in another way. The crime of robbery means the taking of money directly from the person of another, or in his or her immediate presence. It is a felony, even though the amount of money taken may be quite small.

Bribery is the offering of monies or other things of value to a public official in return for a favor of some kind. A variety of this crime is "commercial bribery," which involves the same motive and the same act, but the target is not a public official (it's probably a businessperson). The penalty for ordinary bribery is usually more serious than that for commercial bribery. So, again, the seriousness of the crime depends on the character of the victim.

The most common delineation of property crimes is based upon the amount of property obtained. The crime of theft covers a wide range of activities. All involve the illegal gain of money or something of value. Usually the different categories or "degrees" of theft are measured by how much money is obtained, or how much the thief tries to obtain.

Many states have enacted more specific definitions of what is theft, in light of modern day life and business realities. For instance, the stealing of cable television services, or the use of a "dish" to intercept television signals which one has not paid for, does not directly involve obtaining money. What's "taken" is only an electronic signal. But nearly all states have enacted special definitions of the crime of theft that covers just this sort of thing. This recognizes the reality that stealing the signal ultimately results in obtaining money unjustly.

Sometimes crimes that are commonly thought to involve falsely obtaining property have nothing or little to do with property. Burglary is popularly thought of as a property crime since it usually involves entering a building to steal something inside. At common law, the definition was more particular: it was the unlawful entry into the dwelling house of another, in the nighttime, with the intent to commit a felony while there. The felony was probably theft, but it didn't have to be. The requirements of a dwelling house and entry at nighttime were essential, however. Nowadays, most state legislatures have refined common law burglary to eliminate the requirement that the entry be at night, or that the building entered be a dwelling house. The requirements that the burglar enter with the intent of committing a felony, and without permission, still exist.

There is a whole array of theft-type offenses that involve checks and banks or financial institutions. The issuance of a worthless check may be a separate crime, or categorized as a subdivision of theft. Bank robbery is a separate and serious criminal offense under federal law. All states have crimes defining embezzlement (often committed by a bank teller), or obtaining a loan under false pretenses. There may also be degrees of these offenses depending on the amounts stolen or the circumstances.

Another major subdivision of property crimes is the "fraud" offenses. Issuing a bad check is an example. Other crimes of this variety are "bunco"—the use of a fraud or deceit so mischievous ("sneaky" is perhaps the best term), that society classifies it as a crime. Sometimes the victim of these schemes, a child or an elderly person, is what makes it a crime. Sometimes obtaining a public benefit (like welfare) by misrepresentation is what makes the activity criminal. Believe it or not, there is a line at which business ethics (or the lack of business ethics) can become criminal. Particularly when stocks, land deeds, or other official documents are involved.

A final subcategory of property crimes is those in which no one actually takes the property. It may be damaged—the offense is criminal damage to property, or it may be land entered without authorization—then the offense is trespass. If someone else took the property, but passed it along through a third person for profit—the offense is one of receiving and concealing stolen property, or "fencing."

SEX AND FAMILY CRIMES

Sex and family crimes are separately classified as such in every state. At common law, the major sex crime was rape, defined as the forcible sexual penetration of a victim. Not all sex crimes are rapes. For instance, there may be forcible or at least unwanted sexual activity that doesn't involve penetration. There may be the use of a weapon with a sexual purpose other than penetration.

Some states still categorize such acts not under the common law notion of rape, but have adopted a broader statutory definition under the heading of "criminal sexual conduct." They then further sub-classify the various acts involved by degrees, depending on whether there was actual sexual penetration, or bodily harm resulted, or a weapon was used.

Another subset of sex offenses includes sodomy and bestiality, meaning sexual activity with an animal or among humans in some fashion not thought of as "normal" (to the legislature, anyway). These are not widely enforced, and encounter a host of other problems when they are.

Related, at least in some sense, to the sex crimes are crimes against the family. Bigamy (multiple marriages) is the most widely-known of these. Many states today also have separate offenses for child abuse and non-support of a child or family.

CRIMES AGAINST THE GOVERNMENT, OR AGAINST PUBLIC SAFETY

Another major subdivision of criminal definitions concerns activities that have a bearing on government activities or the public safety. We have already mentioned bribery of a public official as an example.

Treason and mutiny are the most notorious of these offenses, though rarely seen nowadays. Treason means the attempted overthrow of the legitimate government, or its betrayal into the hands of a foreign power. Mutiny means the insurrection of seamen or soldiers against their commanding officers.

Other crimes against the government involve fraud upon a public body (including welfare fraud), or interference with the system of justice such as jury-tampering or perjury. Related to these are efforts to avoid lawful arrest ("resisting arrest"). Also in this category is the crime of escape, typically by a jailed prisoner. Tax violations are a whole separate body of offenses.

Some offenses against the public involve its safety or welfare. Most states have separate criminal statutes for adulterating foods, or placing or permitting dangerous instrumentalities (such as "snare guns") to exist, or dangerous animals to roam at large. Some minor offenses of this nature are of the "ordinance violation" variety: public drunkenness, loitering, or being a public nuisance. The definitions of some of these offenses are so vague that the courts have ruled it is unconstitutional to enforce them; they amount to nothing more than the unlimited license to the police to harass persons for conduct that isn't really any worse than offensive.

Finally, every state has made criminal a range of activities that adversely affect its commercial activity. A truck driver who has too much weight, or the salesperson who lacks a license for what he or she is selling, are examples. These "administrative" offenses often skirt the border between what is criminal activity and what's forbidden without a "criminal" penalty (that is, there is no jail sentence or fine). Still, some of these crimes can be very serious. Environmental pollution of an area can entail serious consequences.

CONTROLLED
SUBSTANCES

Large sections of many state laws now contain definitions about crimes involving drugs. Many drugs are legal when prescribed by a physician but illegal when sold or obtained otherwise. Some drugs are illegal under all circumstances.

Many state laws on this subject avoid the use of the term "drug" in favor of the more modern term "controlled substance." This means that the substance, which is almost always a pharmaceutical drug, is restricted in some fashion. These laws also typically contain a long, detailed section classifying the controlled substances by their pharmaceutical properties and their potency. The degree of seriousness that society sets for possession of these drugs usually depends on their categorization under these definitions.

The so-called "war on drugs" has affected American criminal law in a vast set of ways, too many and too complicated to detail here. However, you should be aware that the present penalties for many drug possessions and sales under federal law are far more serious than they are under state law. They are far more serious than they were in the not-too-distant past. To many persons the penalties have no sensible relationship at all to the particular drugs involved or what is done with them.

You should also be aware that the federal government, working often with state police, has special drug crime enforcement and investigative units. These are set up to monitor and detect illegal narcotics activities. They are well funded and very active in major American cities. Over the last 20-30 years they have been the outgrowth of much money appropriated by state and federal legislatures.

Seventy-five to one hundred years ago similar legislative activities went on, but with alcohol, not drugs. A complete switch in society's view of the substances has occurred. Drugs were a minor problem. Cocaine and morphine were legal, commonly prescribed by physicians, or their possession was not a serious crime. "Demon rum" was the real villain. Today alcohol is sold openly and aggressively, and the pharmaceuticals are tightly controlled.

A series of criminal laws still governs alcohol. Most of these involve the ingestion of alcohol and driving a motor vehicle, although some regulate the liquor industry itself. There are still restrictions involving the transportation or sale of alcoholic beverages, or their use by minors.

Some of these same attitudes and restrictions can be found in various laws involving tobacco products, and other contraband, or semi-contraband.

"VICTIMLESS" CRIMES

Another subdivision of crime, related in a sense to the controlled substances laws, is the so-called "victimless" crimes. The central idea of this classification is that society regards some actions of an individual as society's business, though no one is hurt, except perhaps for the criminal himself or herself. Most of these involve some kind of vice or peccadillo.

Probably the most common of these offenses, though maybe not the most commonly-prosecuted, are the gambling offenses. These crimes take on categorization and definitions with a logic that defies explanation. What is criminal on one piece of property is perfectly legal (and advertised and promoted) on another.

Prostitution is another offense in this category. Again, in some places it is perfectly legal. In most, however, it is forbidden, though poorly enforced.

Some criminal offenses involve the simple possession of an item, such as obscene literature. Others involve the doing of an otherwise legal act to excess—public drunkenness, for example. These offenses are usually minor. With a change in circumstances, though, they can be very major offenses with very major consequence. Witness the very serious federal penalties for interstate bookmaking.

ANTICIPATORY
CRIMES

There are many activities done with the intent to commit a crime, but which are not ordinarily thought of as criminal, or which result only in a failed crime. These actions can be crimes, even though the effort fails.

The common law recognized the crime of "attempt." This does not refer to simply a failed crime. It means the taking of a substantial step toward the commission of a crime, with the intent that the crime succeed, and coming perilously close to succeeding. There is a fine line between the offender who abandons his criminal effort and one who goes far enough to commit the separate crime of "attempt."

"Conspiracy" refers to an agreement or an understanding among two or more persons to perpetrate a criminal activity. It is the agreement that constitutes the criminal act, not what the agreement engages the conspirators to do, although that underlying act is itself a separate crime, assuming the conspiracy succeeds. It makes no difference whether the underlying crime does succeed. A crime has been committed with the conspiracy.

Finally, there is another category of crime known as "aiding and abetting" another to commit a criminal act. The actor himself or herself does not commit the underlying crime; rather, the actor is the "getaway" accomplice, or helps the criminal in some significant fashion. Typically, there is a lesser penalty for the crime of "aiding and abetting" than there is for the underlying criminal act.

PROCEDURAL VS. SUBSTANTIVE LAW

Finally, keep in mind that the term "criminal law" itself makes a distinction between laws that define a crime, and laws about the procedures to investigate or prosecute crimes. This is the distinction between the "substantive law" and "procedural law." When you're robbing a bank, you're running afoul of the substantive criminal law; when you're prosecuted for robbing the bank, it will be according to the rules of the procedural criminal law of your jurisdiction. Substantive criminal law defines what behavior constitutes a criminal act. Procedural criminal law sets forth the procedures by which the legal system prosecutes a criminal act.

Some states have two separate sets of statutes to deal with these subjects; others combine them into one criminal code. It makes no sense, for instance, to try to find out what constitutes a second degree murder by checking the criminal procedural law. At the end of this book, there is a state-by-state listing of where you can find the major criminal codes of each state, both procedural and substantive.

Beware that this list is not exhaustive. For instance, it is common for statutes relating to drug crimes or defining what is a controlled substance to appear in print somewhere other than in the state criminal code. Also, state and federal tax codes may contain definitions of criminal activities, or make definitions that have a major bearing on what is or is not a crime. Nonetheless, the listing in the Appendix should get you started in classifying the charges against you as felonies or misdemeanors, by their degree of seriousness, and by their subject matter. As we said earlier, having a clear conception of these classifications may be crucial in your defense later.

ANALYZING YOUR CASE

The first thing you need to do to determine if you have a defense to the crime you are charged with is to learn the elements of the crime charged. That's why this chapter and some materials in the Appendix cover the different kinds of crimes—to help you find out about the crime involved in your case. If you're charged with burglary and your local law requires that a burglary take place at night, and the prosecution has a tough time showing it was nighttime, you have a major bargaining chip. It's these elements of the charge, and the prosecution's strengths and weaknesses proving those elements, which ought to be the focus in plea negotiations—not the fact that you're otherwise a charming person.

PREPARING YOUR DEFENSE 6

DO YOU NEED A LAWYER?

The answer to this question is no doubt "Yes," now more than ever. But for the reasons explained in our Introduction, you may choose not to use one. The choice is up to you. In many cases, the decision of whether or not to hire a lawyer is an economic one, sort of a cost/benefit analysis. For small cases, it may not make a lot of sense in the long run. In bigger cases, it makes more sense to hire a lawyer, but there are many reasons why you might elect to go it alone. We won't repeat them again.

But let nothing in this book dissuade you from hiring professional counsel if you feel the need. All other things being equal (and with unlimited funds), you'll be better off.

CAN YOU GET A FREE LAWYER?

The Sixth Amendment to the United States Constitution provides:

> *In all criminal prosecutions, the accused shall enjoy the assistance of counsel for his defense.*

We haven't dealt much with this constitutional right on the assumption that you want to defend yourself. That's why you bought this book. You may come to a point in your case where you feel you've gone far enough on your own. It's time to call in a lawyer. With all the details and the strategies involved, plea negotiations may well be that time. You really don't need a lawyer at an arraignment, where all you have to do is stand up and plead not guilty. You shouldn't need one to keep your mouth shut as you're sitting in the local lockup. But you may need one to decipher the whims and the fancies of a local prosecutor in trying to fashion a favorable plea deal.

The courts have interpreted the Sixth Amendment broadly. On its face, it practically guarantees you a lawyer, and the cases have interpreted it that way where you're facing jail as a potential punishment. In many jurisdictions, though, if you do not want a lawyer, you do not have to have one. You can defend yourself, whatever the wisdom of doing so. After all, it's you who will do the time, not the lawyer.

In other states, though, the defendant who insists on defending himself or herself must allow a lawyer appointed by the judge to sit next to him or her in court. This lawyer probably won't do much other than offer pointers. He or she acts only as an auxiliary. The defendant still acts as his or her own attorney, does all the talking to the jury, for example, and doesn't have to even listen to the lawyer. Still the lawyer's there if he or she does decide some help is necessary.

Lawyers cost money, at least under normal circumstances. To hire a private attorney for the benefit of your case may cost you several thousand dollars. Keep something else in mind in paying for a lawyer: unless you come from personal wealth, or there is something unusual about the case, you're not going to be able to pay the lawyer's fee in installments. You'll at least have to put down a hefty retainer. "Mr. Green" is the first witness your lawyer will want to meet.

If you pay that kind of money, you may feel that it's pointless to do the work yourself. Of course, you may also feel that this is important enough that you ought to know what's going on every step of the way. Still, you don't want to start the attorney's clock running at every one of those steps.

The public defender system might provide you with a free lawyer. Under this system, there is a separate office of lawyers who provide services to poor persons. The public defender system has received much criticism in recent years, largely unfounded. Some of the best criminal lawyers around are found in the public defenders' offices. They handle by far the most criminal cases, and handle nothing but criminal cases. They are often young, which gives them more energy and more proximity to the local law schools where there is much interest in the latest legal theories. They are also very knowledgeable about the different prosecutors and the whims of your local judiciary. In short, they have a lot going for them.

Unfortunately, sometimes they've got too much going for them. Most public defender offices have far too many cases than they can handle. This is the real weakness in the system. No public defender is going to have the kind of time that a private attorney has to in study and prepare for your case.

SHOULD YOU GET A LAWYER'S OPINION?

A person who plans to represent himself or herself should think about consulting a lawyer for an expert opinion of whether he or she has a good case or not. If a lawyer (or 2 or 3 lawyers) feel you should win, maybe you can do it yourself, but if the lawyer feels you should just plead guilty you should have second thoughts about your belief that you will get off scott-free. You shouldn't expect free advice, but should offer to pay for a consultation.

I'm often asked for a quick consult as a practicing attorney, and as often as not, I'll give it, sometimes for free. Of course, it makes a difference how much time and effort is involved, what's at stake, and who's doing the asking. But most lawyers are far more accessible than the general population imagines. It's not going to cost you anything to ask for something for nothing; just be sure that you ask that it be for nothing.

HOW A LAWYER PREPARES A CRIMINAL CASE

In deciding whether to hire a lawyer, you should be aware of what a lawyer typically does in preparing a criminal defense. You ought to know what you're paying for, since it's all done to protect your interests (and to earn a fee, of course). If you decide to defend yourself, you'll have to do these things yourself.

First, a criminal lawyer makes court appearances, usually with the client by his or her side. On occasion, he or she might make an appearance alone, with just the prosecutor and the judge, or maybe a probation agent.

Second, a criminal lawyer does the kind of legal research we outlined in the previous chapter. He or she will do it a lot quicker and a lot more thoroughly than you can. He or she will know where to look and what to ask.

A criminal lawyer will review police records and other official documents. Again, it's mostly a question of knowing how to do research correctly and quickly.

In some instances, a lawyer might gather evidence on his or her own, or direct a private investigator or paralegal in doing so. It's usually better if the lawyer isn't out front on investigations, but sometimes there's no alternative.

The criminal lawyer will interview the witnesses. He or she might do so as part of the file investigation, or leave that to a paralegal or private eye. As the matter gets closer to trial, though, he or she will no doubt re-interview the key witnesses himself or herself.

Finally (although this list is in no way exhaustive), a criminal lawyer devises a defense strategy. Not only will he or she come up with a theory of defense, he or she thinks through that theory and weighs all the facts of the case against it. It doesn't do a defendant much good to announce a defense, and then have all the evidence contradict it. The lawyer's great advantage is the ability to do this logically and objectively. You'll be hard put to do so.

READING OTHER COURT FILES

One of the best ways to learn what might work in your case is to look at the court files of other people charged with the same crime you are charged with. If they hired a lawyer, he or she may have filed several motions or plead defenses that also apply to your case.

In some areas it may be easy to look up other files. If there is an index of criminal cases and the charge is listed with the case, you can just make a list of the cases that match yours and ask to see those files. If they are not indexed well, you may be able to check the case type through computer records. Ask the court personnel if they can suggest the best method for locating cases by charge.

Criminal files are in most cases public records open to the public so you should have no trouble gaining access to them. You may have to pay a fee, however to obtain photocopies of motions or other court documents you wish to take with you.

SCIENTIFIC EVIDENCE 7

This chapter is about scientific evidence, a difficult subject that is often as complicated as the science involved. We have tried to reduce the problem to some general principles that you can easily understand and apply.

Unfortunately, scientific evidence comes up quite frequently in criminal cases—usually in the scientific tests of various items of evidence and the conclusions drawn from them. There is a whole branch of medicine, forensic medicine, which addresses issues such as how a wound or dead body suggests the way a crime was committed, or what chemical tests show about an alleged narcotic drug, and how that kind of evidence is presented in a courtroom.

We have chosen two cases to illustrate the problem: a drunk driving case with a breath test, and a speeding case where the only evidence is that of a radar gun. Both cases are generally misdemeanors, and each is the sort of case in which the defendant often chooses to go *pro se*. Hopefully, the principles we've drawn from these two examples will help if you run into other kinds of scientific evidence.

DRUNK DRIVING

Many drunk driving cases start this way: A police officer or highway patrol officer notices a driver swerving back and forth on the highway. He or she follows the vehicle, maybe only a short distance, as it weaves between lanes, or in and out of its own lane. Maybe it crosses over the fog line, or goes too fast or too slow for conditions. The officer decides to pull over the vehicle and comes up to the driver's window. There he or she spots common indicators of drunkenness: slurred speech, the smell of alcohol, bloodshot eyes, an unsteady gaze. The officer then has the driver perform field sobriety tests: reciting the alphabet, subtracting backwards from 100, walking a line heel-to-toe, one-legged stand, blind nose touch test, etc. If this confirms to him that alcohol is involved, he will take the driver into the station house. (First, he might administer a *preliminary breath test* in the squad car to confirm his suspicions.)

Up to this point the officer's suspicions rest only on his perceptions (the *preliminary breath test* won't be admissible evidence in court). As such, the defendant can attack his conclusions on the usual grounds: bias, misperception, misinterpretation, confusion, etc. It doesn't take much to fumble in reciting the alphabet backwards (try it while sober), or falling when trying to stand on one foot (try again). If the driver had done these things, it hardly establishes proof of intoxication beyond a reasonable doubt.

THE BREATH ANALYZER

Now for the bad news. At the station house, there is the most damning test of all: the breath analyzer. This device supposedly measures *blood alcohol concentration* (BAC) by testing breath. In most jurisdictions, the driver also has the option of urinalysis or a blood test. Due to logistical difficulties connected with those, and the embarrassment and confusion that's involved, most persons choose the breath test. As it turns out, this is the easiest test to attack.

All breath analyzers do the same thing. The driver blows into a vial. The device supposedly measures the concentration of alcohol in this breath sample. From this, the alcohol concentration in the subject's blood, his or her *blood alcohol concentration*, is computed.

None of the breath analyzer devices measures anything about the blood directly. They measure qualities of the breath sample, and correlate that into qualities of the blood. Most state statutes define the crime of drunk driving as driving a motor vehicle with a *blood alcohol concentration* or BAC above some standard (usually 0.08 or 0.10 parts of 100). In other words, it's not illegal to drive with alcohol in your *breath*. What is illegal is driving with too much alcohol in your *blood*. However, some states have amended their laws to define the crime of drunk driving to include a breath alcohol level.

HENRY'S LAW

How do we get from breath to blood? Years ago, an English scientist, William Henry, discovered what he thought was a fundamental law of nature—that, at a constant temperature, the concentration of a gas dissolved in a liquid is proportional to concentration of the same gas in the air directly above the liquid. In the drunk driver situation Henry's Law means this: if there is a greater alcohol concentration in the blood, there is a greater alcohol concentration in the lungs where the same blood contacts the air.

Henry's Law, like many scientific principles, results in some numbers. Tests do confirm it. They show that the ratio of gas in the air to gas in the blood is a constant 2100 to 1 at a constant temperature of 34 degrees centigrade, which is about the temperature of exhaled air. In other words, 2100 milliliters of air from the lungs have the same qualities, or proportion of gases, as 1 milliliter of blood that flows through the lungs.

But other scientific tests cast some doubt. They suggest that the supposedly-constant ratio varies from individual to individual. It tends to be higher in healthy males than in females. It tends to be higher in persons with a fever. In many people, there is a substantial discrepancy between what is predicted by Henry's Law and the actual concentrations of alcohol in blood and breath samples. For about 14% of the population, the 2100:1 ratio gives a falsely high reading.

It is rare that a highway patrol officer takes the temperature of the person providing the breath sample. It's even rarer that the person reading the test varied the results to factor in the sex or weight of the person tested.

MACHINE-SPECIFIC PROBLEMS

The breath analyzer device comes in several varieties. An older version is the *gas chromatograph*. This is typically a rather tinny-looking box. It runs the air sample through a column of liquid that separates it into its component chemical compounds. Gas chromatography is a poor test for finding alcohol, but it is an excellent test for measuring the difference in the amount of alcohol in two different samples. So the alcohol concentration in the test sample is compared to that in another sample.

The descendants of the gas chromatograph at least look more like scientific instruments. They have gauges to read, lights that blink, etc. Yet each has special problems of its own.

The most common device works on the principle of infrared absorption. A beam of infrared radiation passes through the breath sample of deep lung air. The amount of radiation absorbed by the alcohol in that sample is directly proportional to the alcohol concentration in the solution. (This scientific principle is called, oddly enough, *Beer's Law*, after its discoverer.) From these readings, the device figures out breath alcohol concentration, and by application of Henry's Law, blood concentration or BAC.

This device also works on the principle that alcohol absorbs radiation of a certain wave length. It just so happens that other substances also absorb radiation at that wave length. So the device can't distinguish between alcohol and these other substances, one of which happens to be benzine, a prime ingredient in pain relievers.

A third type of breath analyzer is the *photometric device*, which measures the intensity of light cast on a surface. Less light will be cast if it passes through a medium first. If that medium is a liquid containing oxidized alcohol, even less light will be cast. These devices have ampoules, glass containers that hold chemical solutions. The subject's breath will be placed into one of these ampoules, where any alcohol in it will oxidize; the other ampoule contains a comparison solution. Breath alcohol concentration is determined by comparing the light intensities passing through these two solutions; this is then converted to BAC using Henry's Law.

Photometric devices are not immune to problems. The reagent in the test ampoule is usually potassium dichromate. This chemical reacts not only with alcohol but with many other materials, including household products, prescription drugs and sometimes the breath of sober diabetics.

PROBLEMS IN
ADMINISTRATION

The subject has to exhale enough air for any breath analyzer to work properly. The gas chromatograph requires less air to sample than the other two varieties. It's possible to find a major difference in two samples from the same person, so the testing officer should obtain at least two samples of air from a suspect driver.

The test fails when it measures something other than air from the lungs. That something else is usually air from the mouth, which contains excessive amounts of alcohol within fifteen minutes after the last drink, but just about no alcohol after that. The smart technician will therefore watch the subject for fifteen minutes before administering the test. He or she will make sure nothing goes in or out of the mouth. When the technician administers the test, he or she will make sure the subject breathes deeply before expelling into the collection device; this insures that lung air is tested.

Any electromagnetic wave, such as the FM signal from a police transmitter, can interfere with proper operation of electrical equipment—including all breath testing devices. It's possible to eliminate these waves in pristine laboratory conditions, but not at all possible at the station houses.

RADAR

Our second case imagines an automobile coming down the street. A police radar device records it as speeding. Assume further that the driver sees the squad car and immediately slows. At this point the dozing police officer awakens (the device has alerted him or her), and makes the pinch, but the officer never saw the driver speeding. The only evidence of speeding is the reading of the radar device.

The British developed radar during World War II to monitor incoming enemy aircraft; there is probably no more commonly-accepted scientific measurement in the courtroom. It rests on a scientific law known as the Doppler principle, which is best known for explaining why the pitch of an oncoming train whistle gets louder as it comes closer, but dramatically drops off after it passes the observer. The Doppler principle itself is grounded on another law of nature: that the speed of light (or any electromagnetic wave; light moves at about 186 thousand miles per second) is much greater than the speed of any human-powered vehicle.

Let's imagine that the patrol car in our scenario is stationary. So it's running at 0 miles per second. That makes the mathematics involved much simpler, and makes the radar itself much more accurate. This stationary source emits a radar wave of a known frequency, traveling at the speed of light. This wave bounces off the moving automobile and travels back, still at the speed of light, to the squad car, but at a different frequency. The difference between these two frequencies, of the emitting wave and the reflected wave is the Doppler shift. The difference is a number that, when plugged into a series of mathematical equations, results in another number that is the speed of the moving vehicle.

TARGET RANGE   Every radar gun has a particular target range. That range will be different for approaching vehicles than for receding vehicles. It will be different between devices of the same make and model, and different depending on terrain or weather. It will vary depending on target vehicle sizes and speeds. The range is greater for a large truck than for a smaller vehicle. So the gun doesn't necessarily mark the correct speed of any vehicle, even within its range. It depends on many factors.

TUNING FORKS

Tuning forks enable an operator to correct possible problems in the radar device. Tuning forks function here much like they do with a piano and, as with the piano, they don't necessarily perfect the device. They have about a 10% error built in.

There are usually several forks to a set. When held in front of the radar and properly struck, the fork should interfere with a radar signal at that frequency. Each fork works only for a specific speed. It's just not possible to have enough tuning forks available to most officers to verify all speeds.

The experienced radar operator uses a tuning fork both before and after corralling a speeder to verify accuracy. Still, he or she can only verify some speeds.

OTHER LIMITATIONS OF RADAR

Typically the radar gun has a display that shows the speed of the vehicle. This display updates about once a second. (It's this display that "locks in," so the officer can show it to the violator and persuade him or her to swallow the ticket.) Over about ten seconds the display creates a "target tracking history." It's this history that accurately measures the speed, not just a single displayed number. All police radars have at least one speed display window. Some have more than one. In some states, single window moving radar devices are discouraged, if not prohibited.

Radar, like breath testing devices, is subject to electrical, magnetic and radio interference. There may be false readings due to a low voltage in the radar device itself. Large objects, such as billboards, bridges, etc., can affect it. If the emitting signal is reflected off one of these objects, an inaccurate reading will display.

Radar is also subject to factors inside the patrol car, such as heating or air conditioning fans, or whether they are mounted on a plastic or metal dashboard.

As we noted, the mathematics of radar is different for the moving squad car than for the stationary one; that speed also influences the impact of large objects on the gun's accuracy. Furthermore, if the gun is not in a direct line with the speeding vehicle (say it's off to the side of the road) additional mathematics are needed to accurately measure speed.

A trained radar operator can make adjustments for all these factors, but not all do.

GENERAL PRINCIPLES

Now we have outlined two criminal cases using scientific evidence. Does this discussion of the science behind them suggest any lines of attack on the scientific evidence itself? Not only does it do that, it illustrates some general principles for dealing with any scientific evidence in the courtroom.

1. You have to understand the science that's behind the test that threatens you. All science has limitations. It's those limitations that provide you with avenues of escape. We have described some limitations of breath analyzers and radar devices in this chapter. Every scientific test or piece of scientific evidence has them.

   By resting all or part of a case on scientific evidence, your prosecutor is trying to persuade the jury with a "Mr. Wizard" approach. He or she is arguing that you are guilty because, well, some guys in lab coats have devised a test that says, in effect, that you are guilty. Maybe those lab guys aren't working with "laws of nature" that are as 100% guaranteed accurate as your prosecutor would like everyone to imagine. At first glance, the science sounds impressive. Look a little farther, though, and it may not be the overwhelming evidence it's touted to be.

Studying science is not all that difficult. Natural curiosity will take you a long way. Yet it does mean you will have to get to a library or other source of information, and spend time and mental effort. If you are not willing to do this much studying, you're not going to be able to find the limitations in the science.

An added danger to a half-hearted effort: Your efforts could backfire. You will only succeed in making these scientific rules look more accurate than they actually are.

2. Decide if it is worth attacking the evidence. The science involved in our two scenarios is obviously important. Science furnishes the central piece of evidence in each case. You must attack it to have any hope of acquittal. Not every item of scientific evidence is so important. If it's not, don't waste your time with all this studying.

3. You must study not only the science, but also the background of your particular situation. You might not be able to attack the scientific principles behind radar, but you might sow some doubt by looking into the target range and tuning forks of your particular radar gun.

A thorough examination of the facts of your case will also help you avoid stepping inadvertently into the deep end of the pool. For instance, it won't do you much good to attack breath analyzer results on the basis that you're a diabetic, if your breath alcohol was measured with a gas chromatograph, which isn't affected by diabetic breath.

4. Pay special attention to the mathematics in these scientific principles. Using different numbers in a mathematical formula often produces dramatically different test results. If it's more reasonable to use a ratio of 2200:1 than 2100:1 in Henry's Law (perhaps you had a fever on the day in question), then the resulting BAC will be much different.

Sometimes the best way to do this is to start with the result you want to achieve, and play with the formulas to work backward to the basic data you need in the first place. Then all you need to do is to justify changing the basic data. Most of these mathematical formulas aren't complicated. They usually call for high school algebra, seldom college calculus.

5. Don't underestimate the value of confusion. Just because you know all about the Doppler shift, and could pass the radar certification test yourself, doesn't mean your average Joe on the jury can do so. A painstaking cross-examination about the mathematics involved, formula-by-formula, might so baffle and bedevil a juror that he or she will have some serious doubts about anybody's capacity to understand this stuff. Those doubts on the juror's part might just translate into reasonable doubt for you.

6. Testing and product improvements go on all the time. So the information you may find in your scientific sources might be dated. You may have had the bad luck of being tested by the latest and greatest product on the market. Check on the latest updates.

7. No device is any better than the operator who uses it. Check on your tester. Is he or she certified? For this machine? When was he or she last retested?

8. Don't overlook the visual impact of the scientific testing device itself. The looks of many a gas chromatograph, even one with a perfect record, probably won't impress a jury if you subpoena it into the courtroom. They might just think this piece of junk couldn't measure rainfall by the foot. Beware, though. A device which uses infrared absorption or a photometric device probably will impress them. Some look like they came right out of *Star Wars*.

9. Radar and the breath test devices have been around a long while, and most judges just assume the "laws of nature" they're based on are true. But not all scientific tests have this longevity—especially recent breakthroughs in DNA tests, CAT scans, etc.

You might persuade your judge that he or she shouldn't admit evidence based on matters that are under intense debate in the scientific community right now. Argue that the fact that a test is new is good reason to look critically on it. Remember, the finest medical minds in the world were bleeding their patients not that long ago.

You will probably have at least two, and maybe several, opportunities to make presentations in the courtroom. These are arguments: you stand up and tell the judge or jury why you're not guilty, or debate another issue.

Please note making an argument, whenever it's done, is not the same as "telling your side of the story." If you have taken the oath, and start telling what happened, it's "giving testimony" and not "making an argument." Showing the judge that you understand this important difference is probably the one thing you can do to prove that you as a lay person deserve to be taken seriously in representing yourself.

You make some arguments to the judge alone, and some to the jury. You need a different strategy for each. There are other facets of courtroom presentations that we will touch on: making objections, motions for a mistrial, and sidebar conferences. All these fall into the general category of doing something to further your case during the trial, besides testifying or examining witnesses.

PRE-TRIAL PROCEEDINGS 8

Processing the case against you in court will involve several hearings before the actual trial. You will be present at all of them, most likely, since you have a constitutional right to be in court when your case comes up. Each of these court appearances has a specific purpose that we will describe in this chapter.

THE ARRAIGNMENT; FIRST APPEARANCE

We've already described the first appearance you'll make in court (see Chapter 4). That hearing may or may not be combined with an arraignment, which is the hearing where you get to hear the judge say "How Do You Plead?" You then say "Not Guilty" or "Guilty." In states where you do not make a plea at the first appearance, you will make two appearances: one for the first appearance and the other for the arraignment.

Most arraignments are perfunctory and take only a few minutes to accomplish. Sometimes the judge reads the charges to the defendant in open court. If you have a copy of the complaint or indictment, you can probably waive this reading and save yourself the embarrassment.

The Pre-Trial Conference; Probable Cause Hearing

In all states there is a series of hearings and conferences before trial. Sometimes these accomplish little except to give both sides an opportunity to negotiate a plea (see Chapter 9). You or your prosecutor may want to try your case. Rest assured that the criminal law "bureaucracy" (that is, the judge and the administrative staff in the courthouse) does not. They will force you and the prosecution to meet at least once, and probably several times before trial. Their objective in doing this is to help or make you negotiate a plea deal.

Your state may have a special hearing known as the probable cause hearing. This may be done in place of a preliminary hearing (see below). As such, it's much less helpful to a defendant. The judge reads the complaint and the police reports, and any other paperwork he or she has about the case. He or she decides if there is enough evidence against you to require you to face a full trial on the charges.

Unless the prosecution has done a terrible job at getting its paperwork together, most judges will decide this issue against you. You must stand trial before you see anything from the witnesses against you except what's in those police reports. You have no chance to cross-examine the prosecution's witnesses, and maybe no chance to call witnesses of your own.

There isn't much you can do about this procedure if your state has adopted it. Go to the probable cause hearing expecting to lose.

The Preliminary Hearing

At common law, there was a different procedure to decide if there was probable cause for a defendant to stand trial. This was the preliminary hearing, and it served as a sort of mini-trial. Many states still use it.

(Most of the courtroom proceedings you used to see on the old Perry Mason television show were not trials before a jury. They were preliminary hearings under California procedures.)

At the preliminary hearing, the prosecution must produce witnesses against you. It doesn't have to call everyone as a witness who will be a witness at trial. It only has to call enough witnesses, and present enough evidence, to convince the judge that you should stand trial. In other words, it accomplishes the same thing as the probable cause hearing.

For that reason, many states have replaced the preliminary hearing with the probable cause hearing. That saves both time and money, but it takes away a very useful tool for the defendant.

Nonetheless, the preliminary hearing still exists in the federal system and in some states. It is a boon to the defendant. By producing witnesses, the prosecutor will preview much of what his or her case against you will be. The prosecutor doesn't have to present everything, but he or she has to present enough to make that probable cause threshold. You, of course, then have a wonderful opportunity to see what the evidence is in advance and to ask the witnesses questions.

During most preliminary hearings, many judges will restrict the kinds of questions the defendant can ask. This is not a full-blown trial, only a hearing for a limited purpose. Nevertheless, the witnesses are there, along with an opportunity for you to discover any weaknesses or confusion in their stories.

The later chapters in this book, on how to examine witnesses or make courtroom arguments, are also useful at the preliminary hearing. Assume it's just like the real trial, though without a jury. That difference is important. It means there's really nothing at stake. You can ask a witness all sorts of questions about what he or she knows—you might find out a lot. If the witness gives you an answer that hurts you, so what? Nobody's hurt (yet), and you can use the information to plan how to defend against the answer at the real trial. Your own natural curiosity is probably your best guide. Don't be too worried at this juncture what the witness says—just ask, even if the answer is something you didn't want to hear. You'll be better able to deal with this evidence later, when it counts—that is, at trial—if you know about it in advance.

MOTIONS HEARINGS; EVIDENCE HEARINGS

In the federal system, and in all states, there is a procedure for a defendant to contest the testimony or exhibits against him or her. This is the *evidence hearing* or, in some places, the *motions hearings* (the term *omnibus* hearing also applies). Now the prosecutor will turn over the results of scientific tests and certain other information he or she has about the case.

There may be two hearings. At one (the "motions hearing"), you can ask the prosecutor to show you his or her evidence, or the prosecutor can ask the judge to limit what he or she has to show you. If this is all that happens, there will be a later hearing, the *evidence* or *evidentiary* hearing, when the judge will decide if the prosecutor can use that evidence at trial. The procedures for these hearings vary from state to state, and be aware that your state may combine them with other hearings. Whenever it occurs, sometime before trial the prosecutor is going to release to you the evidence he or she intends to use against you at trial.

Given this series of hearings, you should be prepared to make appropriate motions and constitutional objections to the evidence. Be especially keen to contest any statements you may have made, or evidence seized in a search.

HOW TO MAKE PRE-TRIAL MOTIONS

Before the trial begins, the judge will hear motions from each side about particular facets of the case they want to argue about in advance. As we said, you will no doubt want to make some motions to contest the evidence against you, or to accomplish other purposes. Do not be daunted. Many things you should ask for in these motions will be little more than common sense.

When you make a motion, it should probably be in writing. Sometimes a bright idea will come to you on the spot, and you can make an immediate speaking motion. But if you write out your motion(s) in advance, they will then become part of the record in the case. No one can dispute later that you made the motion. If the judge decides against you, an appeals court can decide from this record if he or she was right or not.

There is a real danger if you don't object to evidence, or don't make the right motions to contest it. You may face the unhappy prospect that the judge will decide that you waived your constitutional rights by your non-action. Then even evidence unconstitutionally obtained can properly be admitted against you at trial.

The motion should follow the format acceptable to your state. Whatever that is, it will generally consist of a heading, a statement of the motion, and perhaps a section describing your reasons for making the motion.

The heading of motions, and of all pleadings or papers submitted to the court in a criminal case, takes a specific format. That format differs from state-to-state, but it generally begins like this:

> IN THE STATE OF GRACE,
> CITY AND COUNTY OF OZ
> DISTRICT COURT, TENTH DISTRICT

That much simply tells you what jurisdiction the case is in. The heading then typically continues,

> **The People of the State of Grace**,
> Plaintiff,
>
> vs.   MOTION TO_____
> **John Q. Citizen**,
> Defendant.   Court File No. _____

This much tells you the name of the case and its court file number, and the name of the motion. (Fill in the blank after "Motion To" with the appropriate name of your motion.)

In the following sections we describe the most common kinds of pre-trial criminal motions. In the motion itself, after the heading, state your motion specifically. For instance, let's assume you object to using objects found in the trunk of your car as evidence. In that case, your motion should probably read like this:

> *Defendant objects to introducing as evidence at trial, any items seized during the search of his 1995 Audi 5000 automobile on March 13, 1996, on the grounds that such search was done in violation of his rights granted under the Fourth Amendment to the United States Constitution.*

Follow up on this with any arguments you want to make about that search and seizure. In our example, you might argue in this way:

> *The grounds for this motion are: (1) the search was not made pursuant to a warrant, (2) there is no justification for a warrantless search in this instance, and (3) the police lacked probable cause to make the search....*

We describe what grounds or reasons there may be to evidence in the earlier chapters of this book. We'll describe others in the sections that follow. Consult those sections for the particular grounds you might use.

Some judges may expect legal arguments from you explaining your objection to the evidence. They may not care that you're representing yourself. If you don't have any reasons that at least sound "lawyer-like," they may not hear your motion. This need not be anything other than common sense. A reference to the correct provision of the United States Constitution, or your local law, would help at this point, though. If you can point to a reported case precedent that supports your argument, you'll definitely be points ahead. But most courts are going to listen to arguments made only on common sense if you state them well. Try to keep things simple and avoid nonsense and ornament.

This is a common error for non-lawyers to make when they get inside the courtroom. They unnecessarily complicate their defense and try to dress it up with bombast, pathos or anger. This only confuses matters. The judge will ultimately ignore or belittle your efforts. He or she will consider you an amateur.

On the other hand, if your efforts (be they the motions, pleadings, examinations of witnesses or arguments to the court) are simple, direct and show some logical thinking, many judges will supply the precise legal bases for the motions in their own minds.

Your local rules will define what kind of service and filing you need to make for your motion. Service means delivery of a copy of the motion to the prosecutor; filing means delivery of the original motion to the court clerk's office or, sometimes, to the judge. Check on how much in advance of the hearing you have to make service and filing.

CONSTITUTIONAL OBJECTIONS TO EVIDENCE

The most common kind of pre-trial motions in a criminal case are constitutional objections to the state's evidence. If the prosecution does disclose evidence with constitutional implications—that is, confessions or statements you made or someone says you made, evidence from a search and seizure, or from a lineup, the United State Constitution is most definitely implicated.

If this evidence is your confession or statements made by you, contend that the statement was made in violation of your Fifth Amendment rights and the judge should exclude it for that reason. Your Fifth Amendment rights have been violated if the police coerced (in any sense of the word) your confession or statement, or used a trick or scam, or took it after you asked to speak to a lawyer first, or (in custody situations) did not give you a Miranda warning.

If police obtained evidence by a search warrant, or by an unwarranted search of your home, vehicle, or person, or from a phone tap or similar surveillance, then contend that the evidence was seized by violating your Fourth Amendment rights. Remember that the Fourth Amendment requires that any such searches and seizures be "reasonable," and object to it on that basis.

If the evidence was an identification made by way of a lineup, object to it on the grounds that it was obtained in violation of your "due process" rights—the police led the witness to pinpoint you from the persons or photos presented to him or her by some comment or indication.

"Due process" is a type of catchall category for unfair government tactics; the term has a long and complicated history, which we can't discuss here. Anytime you believe the government has treated you unfairly, protest on "due process" grounds. Not all unfairness violates the Constitution, but let the judge rule either way. Remember, at this point you only get to make the motions; you don't have to decide if they're any good.

SEQUESTERING
WITNESSES

There may be many other motions that you could bring under local rules that would help your side. For instance, most states have rules that govern the "sequestration" of witnesses. This means that one party or the other can require that witnesses be physically barred from the courtroom. They have to sit outside, and can't hear another witness's testimony until it's their turn to testify.

Since you are the defendant in the criminal case, most of the witnesses will be prosecution witnesses called against you. There is no reason to give these witnesses the benefit of hearing anybody else's testimony. Try to make them sit outside the courtroom; if nothing else, it will frustrate and irritate them, and that might show through when they testify.

Therefore, before trial (and in writing, as we explained earlier), make a motion to sequester the witnesses. Be sure to ask that the witnesses be excluded from all phases of the case: during jury selection (if there is a jury), during the arguments of counsel, and during the examination of witnesses.

In some states, the sequestration of witnesses is an absolute right. If you ask for it, you'll get it (the same might apply if the prosecutor asks for it). In other states, the decision to sequester or not is left to the discretion of the judge. In other words, you have to ask for it, but it's up to the judge to decide. The judge can say no if he or she has a good reason.

Realize that the prosecutor could be making the same motion, and the court could sequester all witnesses in the case, yours as well as the prosecution's. So if you have a witness that you want to hear part of the case, this won't happen if he or she is sequestered.

SEVERING THE TRIAL

The government may have joined several persons together as defendants in one complaint or indictment. It fully intends to try them together, hoping that establishing the guilt of one will rub off, by association, on the others.

Some states frown on this practice, but in the federal courts and in other states, it is the exception rather than the rule. The danger of this to you as a defendant should be obvious. You've got enough troubles on your own. You don't need the jury to hear all about Al Capone, or whoever is sitting next to you in the courtroom, when it's trying to decide your guilt or innocence.

Make a motion to sever your case from anybody else's. As we said, this is a matter of local law, or left to the judge's discretion. You've got nothing to lose by asking for it.

CHANGE OF VENUE

Another common motion is for a change of venue. This means moving the place of the trial. Unfortunately, this can be a complicated procedure and it's not often done, even when there is good reason for a change.

Venue governs the place of the trial. It doesn't necessarily determine who the judge will be. So don't move to change venue because you've got a bad judge; there's another procedure to do that. If your case has stirred up local publicity, or if there have been stories in the newspaper, you have grounds to demand a change of trial. If you're in an area where everyone knows you or knows the law enforcement or other witnesses, there may be grounds to change venue as well. Small towns are notorious for gossip. Any possible juror will already have heard about your case, and maybe even made up his or her mind. Another scenario which justifies a change of venue is where the evidence will somehow link you with a local gang, or with a group of persons who have received unfavorable publicity. In other words, the publicity doesn't have to be about you directly; it only has to work unfairly against you. Affiliating you with a disfavored group by itself prejudices the case against you.

Remember, that unless you make motion(s), nothing is going to happen in your favor. You have to take some defensive steps to protect yourself. You really have nothing to lose. All that could happen is that the judge will deny the motion. You'll be in no worse shape than you were before. If you believe you have any reason to believe that you can benefit from a change of venue (or from any of your other motions), make it.

REMOVAL OF THE JUDGE

Another common motion is for removal of a judge. This is something governed by local rules. Sometimes it's mandatory, meaning you have an absolute right to prevent a judge (maybe just one local judge) from presiding at trial of your case. In other instances, it's discretionary. In other words, you'll ask a judge to rule that he or she has a bias against you and to remove himself or herself from the case.

Like most of us, most judges won't acknowledge their own biases. On the other hand, many acknowledge that their job is to be impartial and to be seen as such. Maybe your judge doesn't want to be seen rejecting a claim that he or she is biased; it is easier to avoid the problem altogether. So he or she will honor a well-reasoned request to assign the case to another judge. Maybe the judge assigned to your case knows the victim or has connections to the prosecution. That may be enough to persuade the judge to remove himself or herself. The judge may be sensitive to the threat of publicity, or to the threat of review by an appeals court.

There are probably time limits on motions such as the removal of a judge, so you should check it out well before the trial. Often, once a judge hears one phase of a case, he or she can't be removed—on the theory that if he or she has a bias, you should have done something to get rid of him or her beforehand.

EVIDENTIARY REQUIREMENTS

Many particular kinds of crimes have built-in procedural rights for the defendant. For instance, in a drunk driving case, many states require the prosecution to produce records regarding the test or machine used to measure your blood alcohol content. Sometimes the law even requires the prosecution to produce as a witness at trial the person who did the actual measurement of the blood alcohol. In other words, the prosecution can't just use the final report prepared on the test. It must show that the machinery was reliable, that the test was conducted properly, and that the final report correctly interprets the data. You may not really want the examiner in court, but you should be aware that your local law may allow you to have him or her there.

PRE-TRIAL DISCOVERY

Before you can object to evidence, you first have to know what it is. Every jurisdiction has a procedure for the prosecution to tell you what evidence it intends to use against you. You may have to make a motion or file a pleading to obtain it, or your opponent might just turn it over without you asking. Make sure you find out your state's procedure, and follow it.

Demand that your prosecutor furnish you with a list of his or her witnesses, giving you their addresses and any records of prior criminal activity on their part. Some judges will restrict giving out witnesses' addresses, but ask for them anyway. Also demand that the prosecutor give you a list of any documents or other exhibits he or she intends to use as evidence against you at trial. The rules generally require the prosecutor to furnish you with a list of any evidence obtained by a search and seizure, or through a search warrant, or from a lineup, or statements or confessions made by you or your accomplices.

Be alert to the fact that a lineup is any identification of you made by a witness beyond what he or she recollects from the crime itself. It doesn't necessarily have to look like it usually does in the movies. A lineup does not require your personal participation. It may have been a lineup by photographs only, for example.

The prosecution is also obligated to turn over to you any evidence it has that might establish your innocence, or at least negate your guilt. Why would it have such evidence? There are lots of reasons. Maybe the police investigation went down many paths before it focused on you. Maybe such evidence turned up accidentally. Maybe somebody planted it trying to get you off. Whatever the reason, he or she must give it to you.

Most states further require the prosecutor to furnish you with any information he or she has about your own criminal record. Some go further; the prosecutor may have to tell you about the criminal records of other defendants, or of your accomplices or co-conspirators, even if they are not co-defendants. Some states require this disclosure about any witness the prosecution intends to call at trial. This is important information if you are to testify yourself at trial, or for your cross-examination of these other persons.

Your prosecutor has to let you see police reports, and records of tests or other scientific matters. The judge might restrict this for a good reason, but probably not. Many prosecutors will simply make copies of all of them for you. They might even furnish them quickly at the arraignment. These reports usually have little to hide. The prosecutor would probably just give them to you. He or she probably doesn't want the inconvenience of having you come into his or her office and sit for several hours or days going over the originals. Again, insist on your rights. If you don't get any police reports, or other investigative or scientific tests or reports, you're being taken advantage of, so demand them by name.

Put on the spot by a specific demand for information, most prosecutors will reveal this evidence to the extent required by local rules without objection. If he or she doesn't, bring that failure to the attention of the judge at the evidence hearing. Tell the judge that you asked for these items and got no reply. If you made your demand in writing, a copy of that accompanying your motion is all that's needed. Then ask the court to disallow the introduction at trial of any of this evidence the prosecutor hasn't revealed.

A FINAL WORD

Again, we can't emphasize enough that you don't hurt yourself by making motions. There are some lawyers whose favorite tactic is to flood the court with defense motions, most of which they have no hope of winning. Occasionally one of them will bear fruit unexpectedly. Even if it doesn't, just the onus of having the prosecution fight these motions, and having the judge rule upon them, can bring benefits to a defendant. Prosecutors get tired of fighting and judges get tired of ruling on these pre-trial matters. Let them be tired. You have much more at stake.

How to 9
Negotiate a
Good Deal

Probably 95% of all criminal cases end in some sort of "negotiated plea," the result of a "plea bargain." Although plea bargaining has received a bad name in recent years (for many reasons), it is something that you must face in handling your case—even if you have no desire or impetus to negotiate a plea. The subject will simply come up because the prosecutor, at some juncture, is going to want to talk to you about "making a deal." If he or she doesn't, the judge surely will.

What to Negotiate?

The term "plea negotiation," strictly speaking, only means negotiations about whether you change your plea or pleas in the case. Presuming that you have already entered a "not guilty" plea to the charges against you at your arraignment, if you now make a "plea bargain," you will change that plea. You will plead "guilty" to at least one of the counts of the complaint, assuming the prosecutor will not just dismiss all charges. In exchange, the prosecution may dismiss or continue the other counts against you. In a multi-count charge, the prosecution may be willing to take a guilty plea as to some in exchange for dropping the rest.

The plea does not necessarily have to involve a plea to fewer counts than what you are charged. The prosecutor might amend the complaint to charge you with a lesser crime: burglary reduced to trespass, or aggravated assault reduced to misdemeanor assault, for example.

A more common negotiation is not over the number of counts you plead guilty to, but over the sentence the judge will impose. This, strictly speaking, is "sentence negotiations." You are not interested in making any kind of deal as to the number of counts to which you plead. Instead, what you are interested in is, "What sentence am I going to get?" In other words, you and the prosecutor work out some deal as far as what the sentence will be (whether it is jail time or fine or both) and the judge accepts it.

Whether you are negotiating about your plea, or negotiating directly about your sentence, it is probably your sentence that you are really interested in. You should know the impact of your plea negotiation if you are going to do it intelligently. Sometimes reducing three counts to one, or twenty to six, will make no difference in the sentence you receive. It will only "sound better" that you pled guilty to fewer charges.

On the other hand, negotiating a plea to fewer charges may make a big difference in the sentence imposed. To know that, you must do the mathematics involved in all the possible sentencing results. (See Chapter 12.) Remember, too, to compute the potential maximum sentencing you could receive if you are found guilty on any or all of the charges, or you plead guilty to the charge(s) you and the prosecutor have negotiated. You cannot decide if you are negotiating a "good deal" until you balance your risks from pleading versus not pleading.

WITH WHOM DO YOU NEGOTIATE?

The easy answer to this question is that you will be negotiating with the prosecutor—but it is a trickier answer than you may expect. You may think you are negotiating with the prosecutor in the courtroom, but in reality you could be negotiating with one or more of his or her superiors.

Many prosecution offices have policies on plea negotiations. This can make it harder to deal with the courtroom prosecutor. He or she may not have any authority to vary from that policy, at least not without clearing it with the boss.

However, this may also be a sham negotiating technique. In other words, the prosecutor in the courtroom may tell you that his or her office policy is such-and-such just to make you think that he or she has no room to negotiate. In reality, the prosecutor has that room if he or she really does want to cut a deal. He or she can always hoist the blame for a supposed inability to cut you a better bargain back onto his or her superiors.

Sometimes, the prosecutor will resort to the "hidden principal" technique of negotiating. He or she will say that he or she agrees with your position and thinks it would be a sensible resolution of your case, but the "big boss" will not go for it. In order for the prosecutor to keep his or her job, he or she has to do things by their plea policy.

My suggestion is not to pay any attention to claims of "office policy" or the "hidden principal," though they're absolutely true sometimes. Try to work out as good of a deal as you can with the prosecutor in the courtroom. Assume he or she has the authority to carry this deal through. Then tell him or her to clear it with whomever he or she claims must clear it. The prosecutor's job security is not your problem. If the resolution you propose is a sensible one from his or her standpoint (see below), this will work more often than not.

Besides dealing with the prosecutor, you may also do some negotiating with the judge. In fact, one of the prosecutor's favorite tricks, when something cannot be negotiated, is to propose this: "We cannot agree on that, so let's just leave it to the judge's discretion." This leads you to believe that you will get a better deal from the judge than you would from the prosecutor directly. You might or you might not. I suggest you consider who your judge is (and read the section of this book on removing the judge), before agreeing to any such thing.

Another body that you may have to negotiate with, although you think you are dealing only with the prosecutor, is the local parole or probation office. Often the prosecutor may try to leave troublesome details to that office, which routinely advises the judge on sentencing. When that happens, I suggest you check with the office that's involved directly. Try to find out as much as you can about the likely outcome of your plea deal before you put your John Hancock on any plea agreement.

Finally, you may have to negotiate with the victim of the crime, although indirectly. Many jurisdictions have enacted laws that give the victim of a crime the right to be present when a plea deal is being struck. Sometimes the victim can veto a proposed plea to a lesser charge.

In such instances, the prosecutor will be under much political pressure to honor (or at least, to not irritate) the wishes of the crime victim. After all, this person has shown enough interest in the case to find his or her way into the courtroom. The victim could be the kind of person who could find his or her way to the local newspaper office if he or she does not like the plea deal that has been struck. Being a politician, or at least working for one, the prosecutor is very sensitive about having his or her name (or his or her boss') appear in print anywhere near the words "gone soft on crime."

THE PLEA AGREEMENT

In dealing with the prosecutor, be mindful of the paperwork that's involved in any plea negotiation. In many states there's a "plea petition" document that's required by state statutes or criminal rules to complete a plea deal. In other words, you will have to sign off on what could be a multi-page document before the judge will listen to your request to change your original plea.

The purpose of this "plea petition" is to make sure you understand the consequences of changing your not guilty plea. That document will contain a section which describes the particulars of the bargain. It will also recite some formalities that by making this plea you are waiving your various constitutional rights: to a jury trial, to subpoena witnesses and cross-examine them, etc.

If you are at all interested in negotiating a plea, you might ask the prosecutor or even the court clerk for a blank copy of the form plea petition used in your jurisdiction well in advance of that date you plan to sign it. You can then review these papers and answer any questions you might have without having to do it at the last minute, when the pressure of making a plea deal on you will be intense. These forms can be long and complicated, not to mention confusing and intimidating. There is no reason they should derail a "good deal" if you have to muddle through them at the last minute.

In some jurisdictions, there is no set form of a plea petition. Instead there is a document known as a "Plea Agreement." This is simply a version of the printed plea petition form put into a narrative. Although it looks original, it follows a standard formula. Thanks to the wonders of modern word processors, this formula is repeated over and over. In the appendix of this book, you will find reprinted a format commonly used in plea agreements in the federal courts in one area. There may be variations in your jurisdiction but the things discussed in it—the sentence, the plea to which counts, waiver of constitutional rights, possible sentences, the factual background, etc.—will appear in some form of any plea negotiation document.

One final comment on the mechanics of a plea negotiation. As a *pro se* defendant, you should probably make it clear to the prosecutor that it is your understanding that your discussions with him or her cannot be used against you later on. Most prosecutors will understand and honor that understanding.

WHEN TO NEGOTIATE

Sometimes prosecutors try to negotiate a plea at or before the arraignment. This is typically done because of the congestion in the court calendars. Since most cases end in plea deals, keeping your case from going one or two additional hearings before the inevitable happens saves everybody time.

Otherwise, there are several traditional times for negotiating a plea. The most common of these is a pre-trial conference specially set aside for plea deals. There are often too many cases at an arraignment and not enough time to have meaningful negotiations. There will be fewer cases at the pre-trial conference. By then the prosecutor will have had a chance to study the case, and judge its strengths and weaknesses. In fact, many prosecutors will put off any negotiations until this pre-trial hearing.

This all illustrates a central fact about plea negotiations, or negotiations about anything, for that matter: timing is everything. Sometimes, the best time for a defendant to negotiate a plea is when the court calendar is the busiest. On the other hand, the prosecutor at that juncture will try to take advantage of the defendant's fear of the courtroom and his or her natural tendency to "get it all over with." If you think that's happening, you are probably not negotiating your best deal.

This brings us to the time in which the court calendar is the least busy. That's the eve of trial. There's only one case on the calendar—yours. By this time everyone has had enough time to study the case and decide where the opposition's strengths and weaknesses are. And it is the "last chance" on "the courthouse steps." This is often the best time to negotiate a plea. It makes some sense to refuse to negotiate anything until you get to this point. This is especially true if you have some ace in the hole or some hidden piece of evidence that you can spring on the prosecutor at the last moment.

Another good time to negotiate a plea is the week before the "last minute." If the prosecutor has not prepared much for trial, he or she might be inclined to negotiate a result favorable to you, rather than have to spend the weekend at the office. Again, this is a human factor common in all negotiating scenarios. All people, including you, me and the prosecutor, tend to be lazy. Take advantage of it.

It may not make good sense to wait too long, however. A prosecutor who has put in a lot of preparation on the case may not feel really keen about tossing it all away on the courthouse steps. He or she may sense your stalling tactics and not let you strike some sort of last-minute deal. Timing works both ways.

STRENGTHS AND WEAKNESSES

Often, an unrepresented or even a represented defendant will come into the courtroom expecting to strike some kind of deal on the most unrealistic of terms. The defendant thinks he or she can convince the prosecutor that this is all just a big mistake; he or she is a good citizen who got caught up in something unfortunate, but cannot really be "guilty" of a crime. The defendant assumes the prosecutor will recognize his or her virtues, although they've obviously been ignored by the local police, and let him or her off the hook.

This amounts to little more than begging and the prosecutor will spot it as such. The prosecutor will be happy to negotiate a deal—but one advantageous to his or her side, not yours. After all, you are a little too eager to finish this whole sordid business.

Don't go into the courtroom expecting to convince the prosecutor that he or she should simply dismiss the charges against you. Don't expect that your explanations will make everyone see the injustice you have suffered in just having to be here. Presume the police and prosecution brought the charges against you in the first place because they do believe you have committed a crime, and should pay for it.

If you are going to negotiate a good deal—one that lets you plead to fewer counts than those charged and/or lessens your sentence—understand that the only thing that finally counts in any negotiation is the strengths and weaknesses of your case, and the opposition's. (I suggest you grill the previous sentence into your brain cells until they ache.) Everything else is window dressing: your good citizenship, your good intentions, your good looks included. If you cannot take a hard look at your chances of winning, your chances of losing, and the consequences of either outcome, you shouldn't be in these negotiations. Only the big dogs can move through the tall grass.

The strengths and weaknesses of each side's case show up in the evidence. The evidence in the case is not what you would like it to be, but what it is, what the witnesses say, and what the physical evidence and documents reveal. You have to know what these are (see the section on pre-trial discovery) to tell whether a witness will be strong for you or for the prosecution, whether he or she can be cross-examined, whether an exhibit can be attacked, etc. Hopefully you discussed your case with at least one attorney as suggested in Chapter 6.

The Jury 10

The first, and probably the most important, phase of any criminal trial is the selection of the jury. The procedure varies from state to state but generally follow the format described in this chapter.

Do You Want, and Can You Have, a Jury Trial?

Before we try to answer these questions, keep in mind what a jury does in a criminal trial in an American courtroom. Yes, the jury decides guilt or innocence. In a more fundamental sense, though, the jury acts as a "fact finder." It decides what happened, using its own view of the evidence and its own determinations of the credibility of the witnesses. Then, by applying the law that the judge instructs it about to the facts it has found, it decides what the outcome or ultimate consequences will be.

A jury does not have to be the fact finder. Most often, the judge is both the fact finder and the person who decides what law to apply to those facts. It is almost unique to the American system, that ordinary citizens (the so-called "jury of your peers") have the responsibility of deciding a criminal defendant's ultimate fate.

Whoever is the fact finder has enormous power. The fact finder is not bound by the rules of law. The fact finder can ignore the law altogether, if it wants. It can decide to believe one witness, for any reason it wants, and ignore others. Since the prosecution has no appeal from the jury's verdict, its decision to acquit a defendant is final.

JURY NULLIFICATION

The following set of affairs is known in legal circles as jury nullification: that the jury can choose which version of the facts it wants to believe, that it can ignore the law and the judge's instructions, that it can acquit whomever it feels like acquitting and maybe not for good reasons, and that the prosecution has no appeal from any of this.

Many lawyers defend clients based on nothing other than jury nullification, especially when they haven't got much else to go with. They just toss the case up to the jury and hope it will see things their way. They choose this tactic although the judge tells the jury to follow the evidence and his or her instructions only, even if the prosecutor has all the evidence.

It's proved to be better than nothing. Jury nullification has been a reality throughout the many centuries of the common law. The American colonists benefited from it in the King's courts. So did the Puritans, in the Royalist courts (and later, vice versa). So have abused wives who kill their husbands in their sleep. So have cuckolded Texans who walk in on their wives and the wives' paramours.

The practice of jury nullification won't find many defenders among the legal establishment. Most judges won't let defendants use it as a stated procedure in court; they won't even let the lawyers talk about it. Still, it's found some intellectual justification lately. Some black legal theorists have defended it as a practice for black jurors to use when the defendant is black; part of their rationale is that it was often the reason whites in the Old South got off with killing blacks.

The pros and cons of this are of no concern here. We do not care what's morally or intellectually justifiable. We only care what will help you win. For the reason of jury nullification alone, you should definitely demand a jury trial whenever you have the chance. You may be absolutely guilty of the crime charged, so guilty that you can be "let off" only by a quirk of fate. Only a jury can provide that quirk.

There are movements afoot in some states for juries to be told about their power of jury nullification by the judge. Right now this is a political battle and the outcome is uncertain. But the thing to remember about jury nullification, whether the judge or someone else explains it to the jury, is that the jury has, and always has had, this power. And it always will. If in your state the matter can be stated explicitly to the jury, by all means do so. If not, then don't. But even then there is nothing to prevent you from strongly suggesting to the jury that it would be a far graver offense for them to convict you, than it would be to let you off the hook.

JUDGE VS. JURY

A judge acting as fact finder is under a tremendous psychological burden to find you guilty. This is so despite the oath of office and his or her innate sense of fairness. The reasons for that should come as no surprise. The judge deals too closely with the law enforcement establishment every day to be truly neutral. Police or sheriff's personnel are always in his or her courtroom. They bring the judge search warrants to sign; they protect him or her and the courtroom; they are probably quartered nearby; their jail is either under the judge's jurisdiction or his or her decisions seriously affect it.

Furthermore, it is a fact of American political life in many states that judges must run for re-election. A judge on the campaign trail doesn't need law enforcement going forth into the community bad-mouthing him or her for "going soft on criminals"—particularly those like you, who have the gall to represent themselves. In short, it's not the judge who is likely to see things your way, to give you the benefit of the doubt. A jury might not either, but they're much more likely to be the kind of fact finder you want.

There are some exceptions to this, however, as there are to just about every piece of advice in this book. There are some cases that turn on a technical definition of an issue of law. You may or may not be better off trusting that definition to someone whose background is the law. In some circumstances, you might want the issue decided by those ignorant of the law. Maybe you may have drawn a notoriously pro-defense judge; there are still a few of them out there. Don't look a gift horse in the mouth.

THE RIGHT TO A JURY TRIAL

Do you have any choice about the fact finder? Can you have a jury trial?

In all criminal matters in which jail is a potential penalty (which means just about everything above the level of a petty misdemeanor), you as a defendant have an absolute right to a jury trial. Be aware, however, that you probably have to make a formal demand for one (see the section titled MOTIONS HEARINGS; EVIDENCE HEARINGS in Chapter 8).

You might also want to check your local law to see to what size of jury you are entitled. There has been a movement in recent years, due to the costs of jury trials (and the fact that they occasionally acquit the guilty), to limit the size of juries. In many states you'll only get a 6-person jury if you're not charged with a felony. If you're given any kind of choice, ask for (no, demand) the 12-person jury. Since the prosecution needs a unanimous jury to convict you, you're more likely to find a sympathetic soul in a bigger group.

THE EVER-DWINDLING JURY PANEL

The jury gets to its status in the courtroom through attrition. First, the appropriate local official (probably the clerk of court) will summon a jury panel to serve on jury duty. In most places, the roll of eligible voters, licensed drivers and other official lists in your county or jurisdiction are the starting point. The panel will be summoned to hear whatever cases, civil or criminal, come up during the next month or term of court. From there, the panel gets smaller and smaller.

For each case, and sometimes several days before the case begins, a smaller panel will be selected by lot from that larger panel. This smaller panel will be given some general instructions from a judge about hearing a criminal case. You should sit in on those instructions, if you can. In most places, you can't.

THE PROSECUTOR'S ROLE IN THE COURTROOM

This brings up a tactical consideration—whether and how much exposure you should have as the defendant before the jury or jury panel. Use this general guideline: if the prosecutor is in the courtroom with the jury, it is absolutely mandatory that you be in that courtroom too. Any time the jury or the jury panel is going to be anywhere near a prosecutor, as the defendant you have the right to be in the same vicinity. Definitely take advantage of that. Just your being there will keep all but the stupidest prosecutor from trying to improperly influence the jury.

More realistically, this is an excellent opportunity to watch your prosecutor and to learn about and from him or her. After all, he or she has been there before. The prosecutor has a different role to play in the courtroom and, of course, a different stake in the outcome. For instance, in many places it is customary for the lawyers to stand whenever the jury enters the courtroom as a sign of respect. If the prosecutor stands up when the jury enters, you stand up. If he or she doesn't, don't bother with it. Save your energy for more important tasks.

Without being too obsequious about it, a good general piece of advice is this: follow the prosecutor's cue in doing the common things to ingratiate himself or herself to the jury that all lawyers do. Note how the lawyers laugh if something funny happens in the courtroom; or even if it's not funny, as long as the jury laughs. They scowl if something troublesome happens. When evidence favorable to their side is presented, they will do what they can to emphasize it. At the least, they will sit quietly and not be a source of distraction. When evidence harmful to their case is presented, they may resort to all sorts of distractions—or they will try to project an air of confidence, as if to say that this stuff really shouldn't make much difference.

These tactics are used blatantly, openly and without any whiff of guilt by lawyers in every courtroom across the fruited plain. They do them to win the case. You should do the same.

VOIR DIRE

The next step in the process winnows the larger jury panel down to an acceptable size. From the panel finally chosen for this case, individual jurors will be chosen to serve in the final jury. They'll be chosen by lot—maybe even by drawing numbers out of a hat. The number chosen depends on the size of the final jury, and whether any alternates are needed.

First the judge, and then maybe the parties (this means you and the prosecutor), will have the opportunity to examine the panel members for their fitness to serve as jurors. This process is "voir dire," an old French term (pronounced "vwa deer") that has somehow made its way into Anglo-American law. Definitely take advantage of this opportunity to talk to the jurors individually. Voir dire is subject to many local rules and customs as to how much time you'll have, who gets to examine first, etc. In some federal courts you won't examine at all; the judge does all the examination, but will usually let you submit questions for him or her to ask.

Do not be afraid to ask questions, but make sure that is what you're doing. Questions end with a question mark on paper, and a lilt or rise in the voice when spoken. Questions generally don't start with, "I am an innocent person because…" There is a time and place to tell the jury that during the trial; voir dire is not that time or place.

A common mistake for *pro se* defendants is to jump at the first and every subsequent opportunity to tell their story to the fact finder. This usually means they try to tell the jury they're innocent at unartful and inappropriate times. They seem to feel they shouldn't have to follow the standard courtroom procedure of selecting the fact finder, presenting them with the evidence, and finally arguing their case.

As difficult as it may be, you're far better off doing things by the book. When it's your turn to question the jurors, do not waste it by making speeches to them. The prosecutor will surely object, and the judge will surely sustain the objection and cut you off. Not only will you be embarrassed, you won't have the answers to the valuable questions you need to ask.

Another reason you want to ask the jury panel questions, instead of using this as an opportunity to make a speech, is because you want to find out about them. You want to do this because you want to decide if they are the kind of jurors you want sitting on your case. How do you find that out? How would somebody find out what kind of person you are? They might ask you about your job, whether you like it or not, whether you're thinking of quitting, or what jobs you've had in the past. They might ask you about your family situation, giving you that long-awaited chance to praise your fine children in public, or talk about your rotten brother-in-law. Since you're in court, they might ask you if you've had any prior experience on a jury, what sort of case, whether you liked it, etc. Since this is a criminal case, your interrogator would probably like to find out whether you've had any prior run-ins with the local police. He or she would also like to know if you have any relatives working in law enforcement, or in the court system. And he or she would want to know if you knew anything about the case before being called as a juror.

These are precisely the kinds of questions you should be asking the jury panel. Use some common sense. Do not ask embarrassing questions; you have no business, except in the most bizarre case, asking a juror about his or her sex life or religious or political preferences. You'd surely resent a complete stranger asking about yours.

Above all, encourage each juror to talk about himself or herself. If a juror gives a long-winded answer to any question, that is all right: he or she is giving you lots of information about himself or herself. A long-winded answer probably supplies the fuel to fire off lots more questions.

Ask open-ended questions: those in which the juror gives more than a one-word answer: "Why do you think you like your job, Mrs. Smith?" "How did you feel when your husband was charged with that offense?" "Was that policeman fair to you? Tell us why not." And so forth. The more the prospective juror talks, the more hints you'll get about his or her personality. You'll be in a better position to decide if he or she should remain as a juror. If he or she is on the final panel, you'll know how to structure your case to earn his or her favor.

Jury studies suggest that jurors are extremely nervous during the selection process. As such, they hide much information. They also blurt out much information that isn't even asked. You have to pay attention to what the juror is saying and try to elicit information from him or her. If you do not listen, you won't have any idea how to ask the "follow-up" question.

Keep a chart or a notebook of some sort regarding each juror. One sheet of paper per juror is usually sufficient; most lawyers manage to keep track of a whole jury panel on a large legal pad. They jot down many particular pieces of information about particular jurors using their own shorthand systems. It's easy to lose track of what juror said what during his or her examination, or even which juror is which. It helps to take meaningful notes.

STRIKES AND CHALLENGES

When it comes time to choose the final jury, there is a further negative selection process. From the smaller panel you've examined, both you and the prosecutor will have an opportunity to "strike" one or more jurors. In most states, the criminal defendant has more strikes than the prosecutor. Usually, the strikes go back-and-forth—you strike one, the prosecutor strikes one, then you strike one, etc.

The actual process of striking a juror is done on paper and in private. You don't stand up and announce that you think Juror #4, the large lady in the red dress, couldn't possibly be fair to you and you want her off the jury. That isn't going to sit well with the other jurors, especially the large ones or those with large spouses, or those that happen to like red dresses.

Generally, a piece of paper passes back and forth between the parties, so they can make some indication that a certain juror is excluded. You might draw a line through the juror's name or make the notation, "D1" (for defendant's first strike). This process is too subject to local variation to be described further here; read the chapter below on courtroom personnel and follow the advice there to find out what to do to find out about the practice in your area.

This strike of a juror at the end of the voir dire process, for no stated reason, is a "peremptory challenge," because it's final and decisive. No one can challenge your decision. You do not need a reason to strike a potential juror. There is another kind of strike that might arise in the jury selection process—the "challenge for cause." It is not peremptory because it's not up to you; the judge will decide if the juror is finished or will sit. You can achieve a great tactical advantage if you can get a juror stricken upon a challenge for cause because it won't count against your peremptory strikes. If you have to use a peremptory strike on him or her, you might have to let someone sit on the jury whom you could otherwise be rid of.

Having an occasion even to make a "challenge for cause" is fairly unusual and it's even harder to make stick. The only real grounds a judge has in excusing a juror on a challenge for cause is that the juror cannot be fair about rendering a verdict. You can't challenge a juror because it's your opinion that he or she wouldn't be fair: he or she has to admit as much during the voir dire.

When would anyone ever admit he or she couldn't be fair? The answer is quite often, especially if that person wants to get off the jury duty. Remember, this isn't a really popular hobby; the government has to compel these folks to serve as jurors under the threat of arrest, and then pay them to do it. Some people will claim bias because they're afraid of repercussions. Just the mention that this is a drug or a sex case and you'll see many jurors looking for a way to go home. Some people don't have the time to hear a case that will take more than a couple days; they might admit that their personal schedules make it difficult for them to carefully weigh all the evidence and be fair to both sides. Some will have thought this was going to be an easy and pleasant chore. Now they have found that they will have to do the unpleasant business of deciding if someone will go to jail. Some do not want to be jurors if it means sitting next to a particular fellow juror all day.

You cannot find any of this out if you don't ask some questions during voir dire. Don't be afraid to ask direct and pointed questions, as long you do so politely. Studies have shown that the jury bases its decision on the evidence presented to it, not on what questions it was asked at the onset. For instance, "Mrs. Smith, could the fact that you're a sexual abuse counselor have a bearing on your ability to be fair in judging someone who is accused of a sex crime?" Well, of course it would. Mrs. Smith will, or should, answer this question "Yes." Then suggest the easy answer, "Sure. You'd probably feel uncomfortable acquitting someone accused of a crime that brutalizes the people you try to help every day on your job."

If someone denies what is clearly a bias on his or her part, ask some "why" and "can you explain" questions. Just get Mrs. Smith talking; she'll probably trip up on her own answers anyway, if she's talking enough. Or, "Mr. Jones, would the fact that you're the grand vizier of the Ku Klux Klan mean that you might feel a defendant who is black is more likely to have committed this crime?" If Jones denies this much, ask him if he'd be concerned about news of this reaching his buddies in the local chapter.

The prosecution also has peremptory challenges and challenges for cause available. There is some restriction on what jurors he or she can exclude; there are few, if any, on you as the defendant. For instance, the prosecutor cannot go out of his way to exclude every black from a jury panel for trial of a black defendant. This has been held to be a violation of constitutional rights of the defendant. If you feel the prosecution has abused its duties in your case, make a motion for a mistrial.

JURY SELECTION

That's the process, but what jurors should be stricken?

When it gets down to the point of picking the jury, your own gut feeling is probably your best bet. Typically for a criminal defendant, persons who have strong connections to law enforcement are bad jurors. You probably shouldn't accept the wife of the local sheriff. The same is true for persons in positions of authority, or management jobs, or who are used to a military-style discipline.

On the other hand, look for (and ask questions during voir dire to find) particular kinds of jurors. Be on the lookout for people who may feel put upon by the government, people who have a job that requires submission of lengthy and bothersome reports to the government, people who have a resentment against authority.

Younger people tend to be better defense jurors than older ones. There are many myths and rumors about racial and ethic backgrounds and jury service. Many people regard Jews and African-Americans as good defense jurors because they come from groups that traditionally have not gotten a bigger slice of the American pie, or have been the subject of notorious discrimination by government bodies. On the other hand, the myth persists that Germans and Norwegians are prosecution's jurors due to some vague impressions about their group's traditional respect for authority.

I wouldn't trust these sorts of old wives' tales too much. There are just too many individual variations to put much faith in what are nothing more than racial or ethnic stereotypes. Instead, ask intelligent questions during jury examination about subjects that touch on respect for authority, hard feelings against the government, etc. Pay attention to the prosecution's questions on these topics too; after all, he she is looking for a particular kind of juror too. Then rely on your gut instinct and common sense. It's been done that way for centuries.

Jury Instructions

At the end of your case, the judge will give the jury some instructions about how to decide the case. These are usually very important instructions but, in criminal cases anyway, they are usually standard. So we're not going to dwell on them to any length in this book.

Look for your state's pattern criminal jury instruction while you're looking up the definitions of the crime you're accused of, and your procedural law. Ask your local law librarian to help you. Nobody talks to the librarian, and if they do they whisper. He or she will probably be delighted to actually be of service to someone.

THE TRIAL 11

THE GOVERNMENT'S BURDEN OF PROOF

The prosecution (that is, the government—but you should always refer to him or her in front of the jury as "the prosecutor") goes first. It's the government's burden to put forth evidence that establishes your guilt before you have to do anything. This is its "burden of proof." If the government doesn't produce any witnesses to establish your guilt, you shouldn't do anything more than make a motion for a directed verdict (see the section of this chapter on THE MID-TRIAL MOTION).

Ordinary persons who come into court and testify for the government are lay witnesses. They'll probably be in the shape you are in the courtroom. In other words, they will be plenty nervous, or worse. Be careful if you verbally "beat up" on such a witness in your cross-examination. He or she may be the victim of the crime. It makes no sense to humiliate a witness in court, when the prosecution contends you victimized him or her in the first place. The jury will see this as adding insult to injury. The lay witness is often a good witness because jurors really empathize with him her. After all, his or her life situation probably isn't much different from the ordinary juror's.

But the lay witness is also the kind of witness who maybe didn't see or hear quite as much as the government would like the jury to believe he or she saw or heard. He or she is the sort of witness who isn't really sure about details. You can certainly cross-examine on those points.

Do not be afraid to take on a witness who is harmful to you or whose lies you can lay out for the jury. You don't need to show that a witness is lying. Just show that his or her story isn't possible or even very probable, or that believing this version of events requires a stretch. Point out the problems he or she has in seeing or interpreting events. Just as you shouldn't be too harsh on a witness who is likely to be sympathetic to the jury, you shouldn't be too deferential to the witness who does you serious harm. You must take that witness on—it's a dogfight.

Unfortunately, you will likely see the other thrust of the prosecution's case against you presented by a **professional** witness. This will usually be a member of law enforcement and perhaps the very police officer who arrested you in the first place. If you made damaging statements in his or her presence, or if the officer found damaging evidence in your car or on your person, you're sure to meet him or her again in the courtroom—that's where the business about "can and will be used against you in a court of law" comes from.

Professional witnesses are subject to the same rules as every other witness. What makes their testimony so difficult to shake, however, is their experience. They have testified before. They are not nervous. They are going to continue to make a living testifying again. They are far less likely than a lay witness to fall into your clever trap. You won't fluster them with the suggestion that it was a moonless night. They will come right back and say that they have no doubt it was you they saw try to hide the drugs, despite the problem of seeing 100 yards on a moonless night.

Law enforcement trains its witnesses to undergo cross examination. They will answer the "yes" or "no" question with an appropriate "yes" or "no." They won't try to weasel out of it as some lay witnesses will. Every question you ask such a witness has to be a leading question. You should be able to predict precisely what the answer will be in advance. These witnesses are taught to trust their prosecutor. They know enough to wait for their side to ask an appropriate open question on redirect examination, to patch up any holes poked in their testimony by your cross.

Don't be overly concerned if a police officer testifies in full uniform with a row of ribbons across his chest. Check if that's all right under your local rules, probably by asking the judge before trial. If it is, you will just have to bank on the cynicism and savvy of modern jurors to spot what is nothing more than "gilding the lily."

There is a final kind of witness, similar to the police witness and just as, if not more, professional. This is the *scientific* witness. The problems that you'll have in dealing with him or her will be dealt with in the next chapter.

THE DEFENDANT'S PROOF

You have as much right and as much power as the prosecution to present a witness in court. If you do present a witness, though, you have to remember that, unless you can demonstrate that a witness is hostile, you can only examine him or her directly—by open questions. Your opponent can examine him or her by leading questions.

Consequently, you should meet with your witness beforehand, and go over his or her testimony. The pejorative term is that you "sandpaper" or "woodshed" the witness; as long as you don't tell the witness what to say, it's perfectly all right. Neither you nor the witness should be embarrassed about your meeting. If the prosecutor asks your witness on cross-examination, if he or she has met with you before the trial, he or she should answer "Yes." And if the witness is asked if you talked about the trial with him or her, again he or she should answer truthfully, "Yes." If the witness is asked to explain that (a question the prosecutor should not ask, but you should on redirect), he or she should answer, "He or she wanted to know what I was going to say. I told him or her truthfully, just as I'm telling you now."

If a witness is subject to your control (meaning that he or she is a friend or relative, and sympathetic to your side), and if he or she has something useful to say for you, you shouldn't hesitate to call him or her. If a witness is helpful but not subject to your control, you should probably try to talk to him or her in advance before calling him or her as your witness.

THE SUBPOENA POWER

You should be aware of the "subpoena power" that you have on your side (the prosecutor has it on his or her side too). Maybe for a fee of a few dollars, the court clerk will issue you pieces of paper, labeled subpoenas. You need to arrange to "serve" (that is, deliver) this paper to the potential witness. When he or she receives the paper, he or she is required by law to show up in court at the time and place specified in the subpoena. If he or she doesn't show, the witness can be charged with contempt of court, and perhaps arrested—that should get him or her into the courtroom.

In some jurisdictions, you must notify the court about whom you intend to subpoena, before the clerk will issue those documents. However, in many jurisdictions, you can get one or more blank subpoenas from the court and fill them in yourself. You then have someone else to serve that subpoena on the person you've designated. This "someone else" may be a "process server" who will charge you a fee, though some jurisdictions provide free service in criminal cases by the local sheriff's office.

You can also subpoena documents or physical objects into the courtroom. This is usually done by subpoenaing a person who has custody or possession of those documents (and who may not know anything else about the case). Tell him or her what you want him or her to bring along in the subpoena. This is the "subpoena duces tecum."

There may be an additional fee to give to the subpoenaed witness to cover his or her expenses in coming to court to testify. Often the government has funds available for these expenses, even for your witnesses.

Obviously, the subpoena power is a strong one. Don't be afraid to use it for a witness who won't show up voluntarily. It won't cost much except perhaps a few dollars to the clerk or for a process server.

Be aware, however, that if you abuse the subpoena power, the offended witness or the prosecutor can go to the judge and have the subpoena "quashed." In that instance, the judge may restrict your ability to use subpoenas; he or she may require you to clear any future subpoenas with him or her in advance. In some jurisdictions, that is already a restriction placed on *pro se* defendants.

When should you subpoena a witness to testify? You might think it would be a good idea to wait a couple of days until the prosecution finishes its case, but unless you have a better handle on the timing of the case than most of us do, you can't afford to wait. Subpoena the witness for the first day of trial. If he or she proves to be friendly to you (probably by contacting you and asking what this is all about), see if he or she will come in voluntarily when called later. If there's any question about his or her willingness to just show up, subpoena him or her for the first day and make him or her sit. If the witness misses time from work, or if he or she has family matters and things get uncomfortable, make him or her sit anyway. This is your case, not his or hers. If the witness has a problem he or she can whine to the judge, who will probably make the witness promise to show up when it's time for him or her to testify; now the judge has guaranteed the witness' presence for you. Otherwise, if he or she doesn't testify on the first day, subpoena him or her again for the next day (you know where to find the witness), and for every day of trial after that, until he or she does testify.

SHOULD YOU TESTIFY?

Recall the first chapter in which we discussed the Fifth Amendment to the United States Constitution—the one that says you can't be compelled to be a witness against yourself. It means that you don't have to testify even if you act as your own lawyer, or otherwise do much of the talking to the jury. You can still choose not to say anything under oath to questions put to you by the prosecutor. If you do testify, you can't restrict it to your side of the story, however; you'll surely be cross-examined by the prosecutor.

There are pros and cons to either way. There is an old saying that "a defendant who won't talk, won't walk," meaning that if the defendant doesn't testify, he or she will go to jail. However, there is an equally old saying to the effect that a defendant who has to testify for himself or herself hasn't got a chance anyway. There are too many variations and colorations to all of this to give any absolute advice in all situations. You just have to make the decision yourself, depending on the charges brought against you and the way the case plays itself out in the courtroom. In either event, it doesn't make any sense to alert either the judge or the prosecutor what you will do until you have to do so. Neither should be commenting to the jury about whether you'll testify. You can wait to decide when it's your turn.

IF YOU TESTIFY

The business of testifying on your own behalf poses some special problems and opportunities for you. This is beyond the conduct you should exhibit every day in the courtroom.

For one thing, you should address the jury when you testify on your own behalf. You are not giving your testimony to the judge. You are not giving it to the prosecutor. You are giving it to the fact finder—the jury. You are also selling yourself to the jury, so you should use all the mechanisms a good salesperson uses. He or she pushes the product but doesn't overdo it. The salesperson understands his or her customers and tries to win their favor, but not with obvious cheap tricks. He or she points out the product's good points and belittles or explains (or even avoids talking about) its bad points.

Since you are representing yourself, the question comes up of how you do direct examination. You could ask yourself questions and then answer those questions yourself. Technically, the judge should probably make you do that; some probably will. However, most will just let you go on in a narrative fashion. Simply tell your story from beginning to end.

Remember that you will have a chance to argue your case later. You don't need to do it now. It would be improper and would probably backfire. Just simply tell the facts the way they happened, using your good sales skills, and then be quiet. For now you are going to have to undergo cross-examination.

There may be things more painful for a defendant in a criminal case than undergoing cross-examination by a skilled prosecutor, but there aren't many. Bamboo shoots under your fingernails might be equivalent. The prosecutor is going to try to make you out to look stupid, as well as guilty. He or she will harp on every inconsistency in your story, or in someone else's story that conflicts with yours. He or she is going to snarl at you and ask you questions in the most unfriendly fashion. To some extent, you have to sit there and take it. But there are some things you can do in your own defense.

For one thing, don't address the jury during cross-examination. You are answering the prosecutor's questions, so look at him or her. This might keep the jury from associating you with the answers. If you want the jury to associate you with the answer, you would have asked the question yourself. Second, concentrate on the question that is asked. You don't have to answer or explain something that isn't in the question. Suppose the prosecutor asks you, "Isn't it true that you were at the

Kentucky Fried Chicken on the night in question." You don't have to explain to the prosecutor that you don't really like Kentucky Fried Chicken, but the other place was closed and you just wanted a Coke. It's a "yes" or "no" question, so answer it either "Yes" or "No." The less you say in cross-examination the better.

Also look for the wide-open question that sometimes sneaks into cross-examination. As you will quickly find out, examining a witness only by leading questions is uncommonly difficult. It is far easier to ask "what for," "why," and "how" type questions—your classic non-leading direct examination questions. Every lawyer makes this mistake and your prosecutor is no exception. If he or she does, it's the equivalent of fumble in football. Pick up the ball and run with it. If he or she asks you why something was such and so, this is your opportunity to score some points. Go right ahead and eagerly answer the question, maybe looking directly at the jury. Explain to the prosecutor why it really was such-and-so, in a way that illustrates your theory of the case and buttresses your defense.

THE OPENING STATEMENT

At the opening of the trial, right after the jury is finally chosen, you will have the chance to make an "opening statement." The prosecutor goes first. He or she will probably proceed by outlining for the jury what he or she believes the evidence will prove, and outline his or her theory about why you are guilty. Most often, the prosecutor will be fairly unemotional, maybe downright cold. He or she may be brief, maybe just a few moments in a simple case or with a lesser charge.

You will have an opportunity to make a similar statement when the prosecutor gets done. You should probably take advantage of this opportunity. There are many cases in which it's better to reserve your opening statement until the prosecutor has put on all his or her evidence. Nonetheless, modern jury studies suggest that many jurors make up their minds at the outset of the case, right after the opening statements and before hearing any evidence at all. Therefore, unless you have good reason not to, you should probably counter the prosecutor's opening statement with your own right away.

How should you speak? Follow the prosecutor's lead. If he or she is matter-of-fact and brief, you do the same. Your approach to the opening statement, its tone, length, etc., should be similar to the prosecutor's. Stick to the facts and don't become emotional. As the party with a personal stake in the outcome the jury will understand if your emotions come center stage, but try to downplay it at this point. Don't worry about being nervous. You might tell the jury you are nervous; it will make you human and not the dangerous outlaw the prosecutor has just described.

State your theory of the case. Tell the jury what you think the evidence will be, without going into much detail. In other words, "Ladies and gentlemen, the evidence in this case will persuade you that I'm not guilty of these charges because…"

You are telling the jury what you expect the evidence in the case to be. You are not testifying, not giving them evidence at this point. Try to be logical going from one point to the next. Many lawyers repeatedly phrase their opening statements in terms of "We expect the evidence here will prove [A, B, C and D]…" For instance, you might say that the evidence will not show that you were driving under the influence of alcohol because:

A. There are witnesses who will testify that you didn't have much to drink at all that night, and left the bar stone-sober.

B. The evidence will show you that the police officer didn't have a good view of the way you were driving; he or she was just out trying to make drunk driving arrests.

C. The evidence will be that you were driving okay; there wasn't any accident or anything very unusual; and

D. The breath test you took was faulty.

Likewise, in a theft case you may claim that the evidence will not show that you were the thief, or that the prosecution witnesses are not as certain about the identity of the thief as the prosecutor claims, etc.

In other words, the sort of opening statement you make depends on what the charge against you is, and how the evidence is presented. Therefore, review the statute you're charged under (see Chapter 5). Get hold of the prosecution's witness list and exhibits before trial (see Chapter 8). Without these basic pieces of information, you're going to look and sound stupid (and guilty).

In some states you can have the opening statement and the closing arguments recorded. Insist that the court reporter transcribe them if you have this choice. (The reason for this will be explained in Chapter 13.)

HOW TO EXAMINE WITNESSES

WHOSE
WITNESS IS IT
ANYWAY?

We recommend that you make and keep three charts or lists during trial. First, as mentioned before, make a jury chart, showing each juror on the jury panel, noting their characteristics and answers to some of the questions put to them. Also list all exhibits offered by either side, and note whether the judge ruled them received as evidence or not. Finally, list everyone who will be a witness in the case, and maybe some notes about what you expected him or her to testify about, and perhaps some questions you intend to ask.

Organize your witness list like your exhibit list—by whether it is a prosecution witness or a defense witness (or in some rare instances, a court witness). A prosecution witness is called by the prosecution, during its turn to present witnesses, even if that witness happens to be your close friend. If you call a witness, he or she is a defense witness, even if he or she happens to be the local chief of police. In other words, the identification of a witness is decided by the side that calls him or her as a witness.

This is important because, unless the judge rules a witness is a "hostile" witness to the side that called him, the identification of the witness determines what kinds of questions you can ask. A hostile witness is called by one side but has a clear bias against that side. Suppose the prosecution does call your best friend as a witness. He or she reacts in predictably surly fashion, giving information only reluctantly. It is obvious that the witness is biased toward you—then the court will classify him or her as a witness hostile to the prosecution. The consequence of having one of your witnesses declared hostile is that you can ask questions as if the other side had called him or her as its witness. (You may have the same kind of luck calling the chief of police.)

DIRECT AND CROSS EXAMINATION; LEADING AND NON-LEADING QUESTIONS

If you call a witness, and he or she is not hostile to you, you can ask questions by "direct examination." The touchstone of direct examination is that you must question the witness without asking "leading" questions. Your opponent, however, can "cross-examine" the witness and can ask the leading questions.

Direct examination questions, or non-leading questions, have one unique characteristic: nothing in the question suggests an answer to the witness. For instance, if you ask the witness, "Could you explain what you saw on the night in question?" or "What, if anything, happened next?" these are not leading questions. The witness can answer them in pretty much his or her own fashion. In other words, the person asking the questions doesn't ask very much, but the person answering has the opportunity to give a longer narrative. Sometimes direct questions are "yes" or "no" questions. Consider the question, "Is what Witness X said about you correct?" That is not a leading question because it doesn't suggest the answer one way or the other; it is completely neutral on the content of the answer. It could be answered "Yes" or "No," so the "yes" or "no" quality isn't what makes it non-leading.

The cross-examination or leading question is usually much more pointed and direct. The question itself suggests the answer. The questioner does most of the talking during the question; the witness simply gives his or her assent or denial (often by just "Yes" or "No") to the suggested answer contained in the question. "You know full well, Chief Roberts, that the night in question was a moonless night." Chief Roberts will answer "Yes," because you have properly led him right to the answer by your question. "You wouldn't deny to this jury that it's easier to see 100 yards on a night with a full moon than on a night when there's no moon." Chief Roberts will no doubt answer "No, I wouldn't deny that," as your question suggests. And so the questioning goes—the witness does little more than adopt the theory or view of the questioner. His or her answers usually add little, if any, detail to what's contained in the question.

Cross-examination is probably the most difficult skill taught to lawyers. It's the most difficult skill you will have to use if you represent yourself. But when it's done right, nothing else that happens in the courtroom is as dramatic or as effective in presenting your side of the case. You advance your theory of the case through the other side's witness. Any juror would be impressed.

The problem is that most cross-examination is pretty limited. Opposing witnesses are not going to bend over backwards for you to lay your case out to the jury like this. Your opponent will no doubt warn them about this and coach them in advance to avoid or limit it. Many, if not most, opposition witnesses will hand you something, though. There are shades of meaning and soft spots in the testimony of most witnesses, and these should be brought out by leading questions. Don't be greedy—take only so much as the opposition's witness has to give you. You don't have to win the game by scoring a home run; a series of singles is good enough.

EXPERT WITNESSES

Finally, if you're going to take on a true "expert" witness, a medical pathologist or actuary, for example, you'd do well to re-read Chapter 7, particularly the sections on understanding the science that underlies their testimony. Then treat them as you would the police officer witness—get what you can and leave them alone. You'll only lose if you start an argument.

OFFERING EXHIBITS

Offering exhibits is part and parcel of the process of examining witnesses. It is usually while examining a witness that an exhibit becomes evidence in the case. Remember, an exhibit is some physical object. It's usually a document, but it may even be any other physical or "tangible" object, like a photograph, a map, a suitcase, a bowling ball, or lawn furniture. It's anything, other than words, which you want the jury to consider as evidence in the case. You enter the exhibit "into evidence" by "offering" it as evidence. Here's how:

First, have the exhibit marked as an exhibit. Sometimes this has to be done before the trial starts; sometimes it's done during trial. In some states, each party marks his or her own exhibits; in others, the court clerk or court reporter will mark the exhibits for the party. In other words, these matters are done according to local rule or custom. Usually you "mark" the exhibit by placing a tag or stick-on type paper (like a "Post-It" Note) right on the exhibit with its identifying number written in.

Warning: If, in your locale, the court reporter marks the exhibits during the trial, be sure to stop what you are doing, hand him or her the exhibit and ask him or her to mark it as such. Then shut up. The court reporter can't mark the exhibit if he or she is trying to take down your testimony. There is no rush.

The second part of entering an exhibit into evidence is to have it identified. Turn to the witness on the witness stand, hand him or her the exhibit, and ask if he or she can identify it. Like this: "Mr. Witness, can you identify what has been marked as Exhibit #6?" Note that this again is a "yes" or "no" question and should be answered as such. The witness shouldn't do more than that. He or she shouldn't actually identify the exhibit until asked to do so. So far you haven't asked him or her to do so. You've only asked if he or she can do so. (If this is confusing, try reading the last several sentences, and the paragraphs which follow, aloud to a friend; the meaning will become clear.)

If the answer is "No, I can't identify it," you should set the exhibit aside for another identifying witness. This witness will not be able to help you at this juncture. If the witness says he or she can identify the exhibit, now ask "Then, please identify Exhibit #6." He or she will probably answer along the lines of, "This is the bloody glove" or "Exhibit #6 is a letter I wrote to you on October 6, 1994." At this point, don't debate with him or her about the answer and don't ask for an explanation as to why it's important. Don't do anything more with the witness at this point.

Instead, turn and hand the exhibit to your opponent. You might also say something for the record indicating what you are doing, such as, "Ms. Prosecutor, here I am handing you what has been marked for identification purposes as Exhibit #6."

At this point, your opponent (or you, if the tables are turned) has a right to take a good and careful look at the exhibit. He or she also has the right to question the witness about its identification, first asking the judge for permission. But that's all he or she can do right now.

The next step in this process is offering the exhibit into evidence. You simply hand the exhibit to the judge and say, "Your Honor, I offer Exhibit #6." Now your opponent (or, again, you, if the tables are turned) has the opportunity to make an objection. The judge may even invite an objection by saying, "Counselor, do you have any objection?"

As with other objections, the business of objecting to an exhibit is brief: "Objection, what's offered as Exhibit #6 is irrelevant." Most judges won't allow you to make lengthy arguments about objections to exhibits or testimony—not in the presence of the jury anyway. The judge will make a ruling and either indicate that the exhibit is received or refused. (Be sure to mark your exhibit list as "received" or "refused" at this point.)

It is only after the exhibit has been marked, shown to the witness and identified, shown to the opposing attorney, offered, and received by the judge, that the item becomes an exhibit in the case. It is only then that a witness has the opportunity to explain it, read from it, show it to the jury, etc.

This four-part test—marking, identifying, showing, and offering—is taught to every law school class entering a course on trial practice. If the student can absorb this much he or she will probably pass the course. If you go through the process of having your exhibits properly identified, etc., according to this test, you will impress the judge—and the prosecutor too. You will probably get lots of good evidence back into that jury room. On the other hand, if you have exhibit after exhibit thrown out as evidence because you don't follow this traditional test, the jury is probably going to think that you are not playing by the rules, that you are trying to put something over on them. There is one right way to do this and lots of wrong ways. Use the right way, but only if you want to win.

PREJUDICE AND
FOUNDATION

There are some special problems about courtroom exhibits that bear mentioning. Sometimes an exhibit (or actual testimony, for that matter) can be properly objected to because it is "overly prejudicial." A little bit of the exhibit is all right, but too much goes too far.

Photographs are the most frequent example. One picture of the crime scene probably helps the jury understand what went on, so the judge will admit it as evidence. No matter that it's a little bloody. Maybe he or she will allow a second picture, from a different angle. But four or eight or thirteen of the same thing only emphasizes the gore; it doesn't help the jury understand. It unfairly prejudices the case against you. Just seeing picture after picture of the poor innocent victim with his or her head cut off adds generally nothing to establish that you are the person responsible for the separation of the body parts. All it's good for is to excite jurors to conclude that someone ought to be made to pay for this outrage—so why not this person the government has already said is responsible? The proper objection is: "Objection, overly prejudicial," and the proper ruling is, "Yes, exhibit refused."

Now a word about "foundation." All exhibits have to be identified. That identification is made by the identifying witness. The identifying witness has to know what the exhibit is to identify it. That much may sound obvious, and that much has essentially been said before. However, if the identifying witness couldn't possibly be in a position to identify the exhibit, that exhibit is "without foundation." How do you tell if the witness is in that position? You have to judge that by the previous testimony in the case.

Conceptually, foundation is probably the most difficult of all subjects found in law libraries under the topic of trial practice. For our purposes here, just keep in mind the second part of the four-part test: the witness has to testify that he or she can identify the exhibit; then the witness identifies it. If the prosecutor asks the witness if he or she can identify Exhibit #4, and gets an answer like, "No I can't, I've never seen it before in my life, but it sure looks like the smoking gun that will put that shifty-eyed defendant behind bars for a good spell," the exhibit "lacks foundation." If the witness testifies to having been blind since birth, and can't even see Exhibit #4 right now, then he or she obviously can't identify it. It too "lacks foundation."

In other words, foundation is judged both by the text of the witness' answer, and by the context in which it's given. It's not a simple matter; sometimes, you have to think about all the evidence that has been produced so far in the trial before it dawns on you that there isn't any support for the exhibit. It "lacks foundation."

Lack of foundation may foul a witness' testimony, as well as an exhibit. Theoretically, the court shouldn't admit testimony unless there is some reasonable belief that the witness has some basis for testifying as he or she does. Nor should the judge admit testimony unless it has a logical connection to the charges made against the defendant. If witness Smith starts testifying about the chemical makeup of the victim's blood, there should have already been testimony establishing that Smith is schooled in this subject and had an opportunity to run tests on the blood. If Smith just starts talking about these subjects out of the blue, his or her testimony "lacks foundation."

If testimony strikes your gut sense of fairness to be from an unreliable source, if it seems to "come out of the blue," then it probably "lacks foundation." Object to it as such. You might be right.

OBJECTIONS

At this point, we need to give you a few pointers about objections in the courtroom. First, you should know how to do it. All you have to do is stand up and say "Objection, your Honor." Then state your reasons in just a word or two: for example, "That question is argumentative" or "That calls for a hearsay response." In the Appendix, we have included a section on common trial objections, and how to phrase them.

Then sit down. Do not belabor the point. If the judge wants to hear more from you on this, he or she will ask. He or she probably won't and will just rule. If the judge rules in your favor, try not to look too pleased. If he or she doesn't, that's fine too—try not to look or get discouraged. You are not going to win them all.

You will probably know if you are making too many, or the wrong, objections. You will know because you lose them all. Better pull back and rethink what you are doing. On the other hand, you may not be making enough objections if the prosecutor seems to be making a strong case against you. There are certainly cases where he or she can do that—especially if he or she has strong evidence that you are guilty. If you haven't been able to plea bargain that kind of case, then you must sit there and take it. It might not hurt to interpose, occasionally, the catchall: "Objection, Your Honor, that's not fair." This isn't a valid objection and will be overruled. But one of the jurors might just agree with you that doesn't seem at all fair. Remember, these are folks who aren't smart enough to get off jury duty.

If you do make too many objections the judge will tell you, perhaps in a heated manner, not only that the objection is overruled, it shouldn't be made again. If that happens, you will not gain much yardage making it again. He or she might be right or wrong; in either case, he or she is the judge.

Objections during the other side's arguments are rare. About the only objection that has much chance during an opening statement is that the opening is "argumentative." Although it is sometimes called the "opening argument," you are not really supposed to argue at this point. Count on your prosecutor objecting if you start arguing your case, rather than logically laying it out, during your opening statement. If he or she makes you "see red" during his or her opening statement, then he or she is doing the same thing.

OTHER
GROUNDS FOR
OBJECTIONS

The scope of this book is too limited to present all of the grounds upon which you can object to evidence. Your jurisdiction no doubt has an evidence code that may or may not be part of its criminal procedure code. Unlike criminal procedure generally, the rules of evidence are pretty standard from place to place. Most evidence codes are relatively short. Your state's evidence code most likely follows the Federal Rules of Evidence, perhaps with a few local variations.

In the Appendix to this book you will find a list of common evidence objections, and a suggested format on how to make them. Study it to learn how it works, and tie its list of common objections to the specific provisions of your state's evidence code.

If you wish to learn more on the subject of evidence you should check some books at your closest law library. Often manuals published by state bar associations provide the most practical information.

MISTRIALS AND SIDEBARS

A mistrial means that a trial comes to no conclusion. Sometimes it happens because the jury simply can't reach a verdict. Sometimes it happens because something amiss happens during the trial, and the judge decides to call a halt. You can make a motion for a mistrial, to force a decision either way from the judge, anytime during trial.

What would make a judge call a mistrial? Why would he or she decide to stop and start over, after spending many taxpayer dollars? It usually only happens if one side strays way out of bounds: if the prosecutor has made many, many inflammatory personal remarks, or asked many impertinent, argumentative questions, or if you've done the same.

To make this objection, ask the judge if you can approach the bench. This is a good thing to keep in mind whenever you want to come up to his bench—ask the judge if it's okay to do so. Also, in some jurisdictions, it is considered proper courtroom etiquette to first ask the judge if you can approach the witness stand, to hand a witness a piece of evidence, for example. Watch the prosecutor and be at least as polite as him or her.

When you (and your opponent) get to the bench, the judge will probably hold what is known as a "sidebar conference." He or she will conduct part of the trial outside the hearing of the jury. Sometimes the judge will tell the jury to return to the back room and take a rest. At other times, when it is shorter, he or she will just hold a whispered conference with the prosecutor and you. The jury theoretically can't hear the sidebar, though they will be straining to hear anyway.

At the sidebar, try to be concise, logical, consistent, and to the point. State your objection, if that is what your doing. If you are making a mistrial motion, use the word "mistrial" and explain to the judge why you think you have been done an injustice. You don't have to be elaborate or carry on in great detail; the judge won't appreciate it at all. Remember, he or she has heard the same awful things you are complaining about. Besides, the judge has a jury waiting to hear the rest of the case.

When it is the prosecutor's turn to speak, let him or her speak. Don't interrupt. He or she is entitled to get his or her side of the story out and the judge will insure that this happens. Then let the judge make a ruling. These are not situations where a display of emotions or an emotional argument will change a losing argument into a winning one.

The important thing about the sidebar conference is that the court reporter will transcribe it. If you have a valid point, it will be "on the record," whether the judge rules in your favor or not.

THE MID-TRIAL MOTION

The "motion for a directed verdict," sometimes called a "motion for dismissal," is made when the prosecution has presented all the evidence it wants to present. You should wait until you hear those magic words "the prosecution rests" or "the state rests" before you make this motion. (Otherwise, the prosecutor can call witnesses back to produce other evidence.)

This motion is directed at some failure of the prosecutor to present evidence on a matter he or she has to prove. What does he or she have to prove? If you read Chapter 5, and followed up on the research suggested there, you would know what we are talking about. Proof of all crimes requires proof of the particulars required by state law. Those requirements are probably set out in the complaint that has been issued against you. If they are not, they will be somewhere in your state's criminal code. Do not enter a trial without knowing what your opponent has to present in court, by law, to send you to jail.

For instance, if you are charged with a burglary, check your state's burglary statute. That statute might follow the old common law requirement that only a "residence house" can be burglarized, and then only at night. Your prosecutor has to present evidence that you entered a particular building, the building was a dwelling place, and the entry happened at night. If he or she fails or forgets to present testimony from some witness that the entry was at night, you have grounds for a motion for a directed verdict. (You obviously can't make this motion until he or she has presented all his or her evidence.)

An occasional failure of proof by prosecutors involves jurisdiction. He or she has the obligation to present evidence that the crime, or some part of it, took place in the particular state or county in which you are prosecuted. It is not your job to supply the prosecution with this information. It is not enough that "everyone knows" that 72nd & Dodge Street is in Omaha, which happens to be in Nebraska. Your prosecutor must find a witness to say that. If he or she doesn't, you have found the technicality that will set you free.

THE CLOSING ARGUMENT

As the name implies, you make a closing argument (called the "summation" in some states) at the end of the case after all the evidence has been heard. Popular thought (which means television these days) regards this as the most important part of the case. The one where the lawyers make special efforts to wax eloquent. On the other hand, jury studies show that "the close" is probably the least important part of the case. Most jurors have made their minds up long ago. Whatever you or the prosecutor have to say by way of summation probably isn't going to change a lot of minds.

Despite having said all of the above, the closing argument deserves a real argument. This is, truly, your "last chance." It is the time and place to let it all hang out. Have your spouse and children, or your parents, in the front row of the audience, and point them out (once is enough). If the government has marked you out for prosecution or somehow treated you unfairly, this is the time to say so. Tell the jury why you are not only not guilty, tell them they should be deeply offended that their tax dollars are going to perpetrate this sort of injustice.

There is quite a bit of "fair game" in closing arguments, much more so than in opening statements. Now you can be argumentative, and should be. Don't worry about being logical or consistent; the time for that has passed. You can be emotional and should be—this is your case, after all. Attack the other side, if it will help you win. Explain why you are a good person, if you are. If you are not, well, show them how smart you are. If you are neither good nor smart, ask the jury to take pity on you for those reasons. Beg if you have to. Just give them (at least one of them) a reason (any reason) to let you off the hook.

There are few restraints on you at this point, but there are still some on your prosecutor. For instance, it is probably "reversible error" (that means your conviction will be overturned by the appeals court) if he or she resorts to race-baiting or calls you many bad names. He or she can probably get away with some bad names, but not many. Object. "Judge, the prosecutor called me an animal. I am not an animal. I am a human being." There is no point being subtle in any of this. The prosecutor wants to put you in prison!

As a defendant, the judge will probably give you some leeway during your closing argument. Definitely take advantage of it. The judge knows that this is your one chance of escaping that miserable sentence in store for you. Unless he or she is a complete prosecution stooge, he or she probably still has enough of a lawyer's competitive instincts to give you a go at it. The judge wants to see if you can pull this off with the jury. Furthermore, if you have minded your manners so far in the case (according to our instructions), then a few liberties are going to be accorded you at the end. What you sow is what you reap.

THE VERDICT

When it's finished with its deliberations, the jury will return with its verdict. If that verdict is "Not Guilty" on all counts, congratulate yourself (and the author of this book) and go home. If it's anything short of that, keep reading.

There are several important points to keep in mind about jury verdicts. For one thing, the terminology involved is not the same from one state to the next. But the important words are pretty well known to everyone: "Not Guilty" and "Acquittal" are good for you. Just about everything else is not, whether it be "Guilty," "Convicted," or something that sounds like them.

Furthermore, be aware that a verdict can be mixed—you can be "Guilty" on some counts but not others. While it is better to win a little than to lose everything, as a criminal defendant you need total victory over the opposition to truly be rid of this headache. A conviction on even one count will subject you to the continued clutches of the legal system.

Finally, if you lose anything and your state permits it, insist on having the jury "polled." This means the court clerk will require each juror to state out loud if this is really his or her verdict. Now is the time for the timid to be put on the spot. Don't worry about offending them—at this point, what have you got to lose?

Post Verdict

You read this book from cover to cover. You did everything we told you. You kept your composure. You were elegant with the jury, polite with the judge, and properly combative with the prosecutor. You made all the right motions, introduced all the right exhibits, called all the right witnesses. Yet everything has failed. You still lost.

Now you have to face the criminal defendant's worst nightmare: sentencing. Unless you are to be hung, we still advise you to keep your chin up and maintain some faith in yourself. You can endure this. The fat lady hasn't even begun to sing.

How to Help Yourself at Sentencing

12

The Pre-Sentence Investigation

Your sentence will most likely be set by the judge. In a few limited circumstances, in a few states, a jury can recommend a sentence to the judge. Still, it's rare. So forget your jury demeanor, those people are history. Concentrate your efforts on the judge and on a layer of courtroom personnel you've maybe not seen before: the probation office.

To help the judge with the sentencing, many states and the federal government these days require some theoretically neutral entity to write up a *pre-sentence investigation* (PSI). This report is usually a few pages long, maybe longer. Your local probation office writes it—or perhaps a special agency that does nothing but write PSIs.

It is all about you: your background, your education and job, your family, your offense. It includes factors the jury didn't consider but which the probation office thinks makes your offense worse or better than average. What is most important, the PSI makes a recommendation to the judge about the possible sentence or sentences that might apply. The idea is that the judge should have a fuller view of you and what went on, and a list of alternatives, before he or she imposes a sentence.

You will probably need to meet with whoever is writing the PSI at least once to supply background information. This is the time to talk long and loud about how important it is for you to stay out of jail, to keep your job, to keep your family together, to keep from going bonkers, etc. Don't be afraid to mention how poor you are and how you can't pay a big fine. Plus you had a bad childhood, bad family situation, etc. If you are going to throw yourself on the mercy of the court (which your defeat has sort of reduced you to doing), you will first need to throw yourself on the mercy of the probation office.

The problem with this strategy is, of course, that the probation office has heard it all before. Your story isn't likely to impress your investigator. He or she is another government officer, with a natural bureaucratic tendency to pigeonhole you into a category with which he or she is familiar. These categories usually don't recognize individual variations. Nonetheless, the investigator might be a human being first and a bureaucrat second. Anyway, it is important to provide him or her with the verifications he or she is going to need about your job, your education, your family background, your financial situation, etc. The investigator may want to talk to your boss, interview your spouse, look at your tax returns, whatever. Your best bet, all other things being equal, is to cooperate with him or her. If you don't, he or she will just report back to the judge that you were uncooperative and may recommend throwing the book at you.

SENTENCING GUIDELINES

In the last 10–20 years many states, and the federal government, have adopted a complicated mathematical formula for determining sentences in criminal cases. It looks like a mileage grid that you see on maps, and it works much the same way. (See the Appendix for the grid that is used for federal sentencing.) The idea behind the grid, and the mathematics that goes with it, is to standardize criminal sentences. The grid theoretically considers only the seriousness of the offense and the dangerousness of the offender. It is supposed to eliminate factors such as race, age, or economic background. In this way, there will be fairness and uniformity across the range of sentences imposed. Or so the theory goes.

The grid works this way: The offense you have been convicted of falls into a predefined category. On the federal grid, this category is your "Offense Level" and is charted down the left-hand side of the grid. Your "Criminal History Category" is a computation of any prior offenses; it is charted across the opposite axis (that is, across the top of the federal grid). Find where these two classifications meet. That gives a number that the judge uses to decide the length of your sentence, and whether it's "probationary" or "commitment." On the federal grid, this number is a range of months, and the judge typically imposes a sentence within that range.

Your Offense Level is determined by another set of mathematical guidelines composed, most likely, by a special panel of judges and public officials in your state. This group has lumped the various offenses into categories depending on the seriousness of the particular offense. Crimes against persons typically rank higher in this categorization than crimes against property. Crimes that can be split into different level of seriousness (such as theft of greater or lesser amounts), will be further split among the categories. The Offense Level may be subject to adjustment by other factors such as the use of a weapon, or whether the defendant was a principal or only a bit player in a criminal conspiracy. The base Offense Level will go up or down depending on these other factors.

Your Criminal History Score is typically the result of your prior convictions. Misdemeanor convictions usually count for something, but less than felony convictions. In the federal system, for instance, most felonies count for three criminal history points and misdemeanors count for one or two.

Let's use the federal grid in the Appendix for an example. Assume a defendant has an Offense Level of 12 and a Criminal History Category of III. This would be the outcome for the federal crime of embezzlement of between \$70,000–\$120,000, by someone with one prior felony and one prior misdemeanor conviction. This defendant is facing a likely prison term of 15–21 months. This is a Zone D sentence, which normally results in a term in the penitentiary. If the same crime was committed by a first-time offender, it would be 10–16 months, which is a Zone C sentence. Under appropriate circumstances, that might be a term of probation only. The defendant may never see the inside of a jail cell. The final grid number, whatever it comes out to be, is the *guidelines sentence*.

Become familiar with the sentencing grid applicable to your case long before you reach the sentencing. It should be the basis on which you plan your plea negotiations. It is the guidelines sentence (and usually not the maximum or minimum sentence that's set out in the statutes) that will determine how much time you'll do.

Of course, "outside" factors cannot and probably should not be eliminated altogether from the judge's consideration in imposing a sentence. In all states, judges have the authority to deviate or "depart" from the guidelines sentence. In other words, the judge can impose a harsher or more lenient sentence than what the grid says. But he or she can only do so when there are factors, recognized in the law, which justify the departure.

What factors justify a departure from the guidelines sentence? Coercion of, or by, a family member in committing the offense is usually a factor justifying a departure, upwards or downwards. Race is never a factor. Employment may or may not be. Become familiar with the grounds recognized in your state on which your judge could depart downward (you should be able to find this information at your law library) and make your PSI officer aware that you fit into a downward departure classification.

Many judges resent these sentencing grids. They think it doesn't allow them any control to impose different sentences in appropriate cases. Of course it works that way. That's exactly the kind of thinking (known as "judicial discretion") the sentencing guidelines and sentencing grid were designed to eliminate. Still, many judges are anxious to hear a good reason why they shouldn't have to follow the guidelines.

DOING TIME

Criminal sentences amount to one or more of the following: (1) serving time, (2) serving a term of probation or parole, (3) paying a fine, restitution, or some other kind of monetary penalty, or (4) doing or not doing something else. Each of these bears an explanation.

"Doing time" or "serving time" means going to a jail, or to a penitentiary or workhouse or work farm. It does not necessarily require full-time daily physical presence in the institution. For one thing, many states recognize and even encourage a program of "work release." You sleep in at the local jail, but go to your regular job during the day. This can be a big benefit, especially if you want to keep your job.

You may get a term of "house arrest." Today, electronic monitoring devices enable a jailer to keep track of a defendant in his or her own home. These are usually electronic bracelets, computers, phone monitoring devices, etc. (Some jurisdictions make the defendant pay for the rental of this equipment.) This way, the jail can restrict you to your own home, where it is presumably more pleasant to do time than at the state pen.

Work release can sometimes be combined with house arrest: you go to work, then you go home. Pretty close to ordinary, day-to-day living except for the electronic bracelet.

Many states have a program of "early release." In the federal system, it is mandatory for part of the sentence. You serve your sentence (or maybe just the last part) in a halfway house or some similar locale. Maybe you get to go to your own home. The idea is to get you re-acclimated to living in the community.

There are still other ways of cutting your sentence. In every state there is a system for computing "good time," which is time deducted from your sentence for simply not causing any problems. It is not unusual for convicts to have 1/3 of their sentence lopped off for simply staying out of trouble while in the institution (this figure is closer to 1/6 in the federal system).

Of course, you may be unable to avoid an institution; if you "do the crime," it may turn out that you will "do the time." Most felony sentences are served in a state penitentiary, while those for misdemeanors are served in a county jail or workhouse. Many defendants feel a state penitentiary is the better place to do time, though it has more of the trappings of the "big house" from some 1930s movies. For one thing, the boredom of a local lockup is absent and there are plenty of opportunities—educational, work, exercise, etc. In some prisons the inmates publish a newspaper; others sponsor their inmates' attendance through high school or post-high school.

Furthermore, if you are going to pursue post-sentencing relief (a subject not covered by this book), it will probably be easier to do from a larger institution. The state penitentiary will likely have a rudimentary law library that prisoners can use. Other prisoners can probably give you pointers or forms on how to pursue your objectives.

If you have enough sense to be reading this book, you probably have enough to know that you should take advantage of these opportunities. The government provides them to you at no cost.

On Parole or Probation

At the end of a prison sentence, a defendant often must serve a term of probation or parole, or both. Or his or her original sentence might be a sentence of probation only. In either case, he or she is not doing any actual time, though he or she is subject to a certain amount of control from the state correctional system.

Parole is an early release from a prison sentence. It is granted for a good reason by a parole board. A defendant usually has to serve a minimum amount of time before he or she can apply for parole. In addition, the defendant has to show that he or she has been "rehabilitated" to earn parole. The ideas of "rehabilitation" and "parole" are thought to be old-fashioned today. Many people, including the politicians and prison officials who set the policy, have given up on the prospect of rehabilitation of any prisoner. Many states, and the federal system, have abolished parole. They have replaced it with the system of determinate sentencing created by the sentencing guidelines and grids.

During the term of parole, the defendant lives and works back at home, or in a halfway house setting. The defendant must report frequently to his or her parole agent and stay out of trouble. If the terms of parole are violated, he or she is usually sent back into the institution.

Probation is similar to parole in that the defendant is out of the penitentiary or workhouse. However, probation is actually an alternative to a jail sentence. First-time offenders and many misdemeanor offenders often get it. Usually there is a fixed sentence imposed, but it is "stayed." That means it is not carried out. You don't go to jail. As long as you keep out of further trouble, and keep any other conditions the judge sets for your release, you stay out. If you violate them, you have to serve the sentence, which was formerly "stayed," but is now "executed."

It is usually in connection with a term of probation that our criminal penalty category (4) "doing or not doing something else," arises. The judge may require a defendant, as a condition of probation, to perform all sorts of acts. He or she might be ordered to keep away from the victim of the crime (the "no contact" order), fulfill a course of education (such as for drunk driving, or marriage or "anger" counseling), or do "community service" (which usually amounts to menial jobs like picking up litter along the highway).

Some judges can be quite creative in fashioning terms of probation, and most defendants are eager to fulfill those terms rather than go to jail. You should be aware, however, that if these terms are too onerous, you always have the option of refusing a probationary sentence, and having the judge send you to jail to serve your time.

OTHER PENALTIES

The judge will usually impose only a fine as a sentence only for a misdemeanor conviction. If the conviction is for a more serious offense, the defendant probably can't afford to pay a fine of a size fitting the gravity of the offense. However, federal law now imposes substantial, mandatory fines upon convicted drug dealers, along with long prison sentences. The idea is that ill-gotten drug money can be used to pay the fine. This seldom happens in practice. Usually lower-level drug offenders have the burden of receiving a fine they can't pay, beyond a lengthy stay in the pen. There may be a growing trend in state legislatures of imposing hefty fines besides hefty prison terms, though there's no realistic way the fines will ever be paid.

Some defendants come to their sentencing thinking they have to pay any fine immediately. This is usually a misconception. In many jurisdictions a defendant can stretch payments over a considerable length of time. He or she might have to ask the judge to grant this grace period. If he or she asks nothing, the presumption is that he or she can pay the entire fine right away. Again, the smartest way to find out about your local practice is to ask someone else already in the system. On this subject, the court clerk will probably be glad to explain things to you. (This office probably collects the fines.)

"Restitution" is also the payment of money by a criminal defendant into the court system because of a conviction. However, this money is supposed to be paid over to the victim of the offense, for what was lost in the crime, including medical expenses. The probation office usually computes the sum due, or it's part of the PSI. In either event, the amount can be nearly impossible to calculate with reasonable accuracy in anything other than a clean theft case.

Related to payments for restitution or a fine are "mandatory add-ons." These might be small penalties imposed by state law and used to pay for the local law library, or some similar service to defendants. They might be larger payments by the defendant for the "cost of prosecution." Some states require the convicted defendant to pay back the costs the government incurs in sending him or her to jail. (Simultaneously, the government might jail him or her at its own expense. If you detect any logic to this, let me know.)

These additional monetary consequences are indistinguishable from fines, except for accounting purposes within the court system. The "cost of prosecution" payments will probably remain in the account earmarked for judicial and prosecution activities. True fines probably wind up in the general government fund.

How to Set the Stage for Your Appeal

13

Now you are really in the deep soup. You have almost read this entire book, and things are worse than before. You have received a sentence you just can't live with.

This is your darkest hour. What can you do? Don't despair. One fundamental truth about the law business is that almost nothing is ever finally over. Assuming you've avoided a capital punishment (even there the odds weigh heavily against execution), there is always something else you can do. There's always some kind of motion you can make to some court somewhere, some kind of recourse the law provides to try to lessen, if not avoid, your fate.

This chapter is about the most obvious of those avenues of recourse—the appeals court. Actually, it's about what to do or not do during the criminal trial to set the stage for an appeal to a higher court. In other words, this chapter is about how to hedge your bets during trial. Don't assume justice is going to triumph and you are going to win because justice is on your side. There is a long line of famous criminal defendants going back to Jesus Christ and Socrates who learned otherwise.

There is almost always a higher court. Its business is to correct the injustices like you have just suffered. If that court is going to do its job, then you have to do things during the trial to help it out and help yourself.

AUXILIARY COURTROOM PERSONNEL

First, let's go back and discuss something that you should have wondered about several weeks ago, or several chapters ago: Just who are all these people floating around the courtroom during your case? Some of these people seem to have some official function in the courtroom that is different from the judge. He or she wears a black robe and is easy to spot. Some of these other people are in uniform, some are in jackets and ties, or good dresses, and some dress more informally. Do these people have anything to do with your case that is truly important? You better believe they do.

You should get to know these people early during the case, for many reasons. First, for reasons we will explain, they are absolutely crucial for your appeal should justice not triumph. Second, they are a great source of information and help during a trial. Any lawyer who has been in a courtroom more than twice knows that it makes sense to befriend these auxiliary personnel.

THE BAILIFFS   The court personnel in uniform are bailiffs. They are employees of a local law enforcement agency—most commonly the county sheriff's office. Their job is twofold. First, they keep some order in the courtroom. They will tell spectators to quit chewing gum or quit making disturbances, and carry out any orders the judge issues regarding courtroom security.

Second, the bailiffs keep custody of the jury, especially when it is sent off to render its verdict. The bailiffs are sworn to keep the jury in their charge and not let anybody contact any juror until a verdict has been reached and received in open court.

Truth be told, though, the bailiffs are often the leakiest sieves in the courthouse. Many are part-time or retired deputies who come in only when there is a jury trial, and then only to keep watch over the jury. Beyond that, they will help you get coffee or find the bathroom. None of this is tough duty. Bailiffs rarely have to strong-arm anybody. Many

144

are overly-fond of talking, with just about anybody. Sometimes, they will even talk about the jury that is in their charge. Even if they won't do that, they will probably be glad to talk to you about the old days, past trials, and funny or strange things they've seen happen in court.

Since you are defending yourself, you are something of an unusual case yourself. You will no doubt be a source of conversation for the bailiffs for years to come. Think about what that means. These folks can fill you in on all sorts of gossip or other nonsense about the judge, the prosecutor, and the witnesses. They will be glad to tell you if a particular witness was any good or not. They will tell you if they think you are winning or losing. If nothing else, you can educate yourself during the trial just through them.

SPECTATORS This calls to mind another category of persons who should not be overlooked as a source of information and advice, if taken with a grain of salt. These are not officials, but spectators who wander in to watch trials. You are not looking for just any spectator, but those who fall into the category of "semi-professional spectator." They tend to be older gentlemen. They are more likely to be inside the courthouse during the winter; in summer they will probably be outside hobnobbing with each other in the park. It's been most courtroom lawyers' experience that these old gents are a good source of stories and observations about the trial. Many cases don't attract them, but the more noteworthy ones do; if you are defending yourself, you will pique their interest.

LAW CLERKS Getting back to the official folks in the courtroom, you may notice another group of young men and women, usually in their 20s, dressed in plainclothes, but conservatively. Their function seems to be running books or other items back and forth to the judge.

These younger folks are the judge's law clerks. They are usually law students or recent law school graduates. Clerking for the judge is more than likely their first job. Some of what they do is of the gopher variety; some do little more than keep the judge's calendar. But sometimes law clerks can exercise more importance than even they realize.

Law clerks keep the judge informed about the law. He or she will routinely send them off to the law library to find a particular volume or case. Since they are recent graduates, they will be up on all the latest appellate cases and legal theories. During their brief tenure with the judge (clerkships usually last only a year or two), clerks typically start to exercise a lot of power. Once the judge trusts them to find the law, he or she will probably call upon them to write drafts of some of the court's orders or legal memoranda. He or she will use them as sounding boards for decisions, or test out language or decisions on them before announcing them in court. Some clerks even get to the point where the judge depends on them to decide the motions before him or her.

Law clerks are tougher to get to know than other courtroom personnel because they don't always deal directly with the parties. If they do, it's only in an official setting. Still, try to ingratiate yourself with them—remember, they are almost "just kids." And continue on your course of exercising courtesy and common sense in handling your case. Learn their names and seek their help. Flattery can still get you a long way, and at this stage you might need all the help you can get.

COURT CLERKS
You might also notice other people in the courtroom whose job seems to be dealing with the mass of paperwork that floats in and out. These personnel are "court clerks" or "court administrators." They may have some functions similar to the law clerks, such as keeping the judge's calendar. They are more likely to deal directly with people coming in and out of the courtroom, and the paper they bring or take with them.

Unlike the law clerks, court clerks don't work directly for the judge as such. They work for a central office in the courthouse. Their basic job is to keep track of the court files. Their most important function during your case is to keep track of the letters, motions, and other papers or objects each side wants the judge to see.

The most important of these "other papers or objects" are the "exhibits." If you ask the court to accept a document (or a physical object, such as a gun or a blood sample) for the jury to consider in rendering its verdict, that object is an official "exhibit." The judge may agree and accept or "receive" the exhibit; if it's not proper evidence, he or she will decline your offer and "refuse" the exhibit. Whether it's "received" or "refused," the court clerk will make a note about it and add it to the list of exhibits. You should be doing the same thing during trial—keep a list of exhibits and jot down whether they have been "received" or "refused."

When the jury begins its deliberations, the court clerk will turn over these exhibits to the bailiffs to give to the jury. Then make sure your lists jive with the clerk's. If not, bring it to the judge's attention. If it's okay, hang onto your list—you may need it later.

THE COURT
REPORTER

Next we come to the person messing with that funny little typewriter-like machine during all the courtroom proceedings. This is the court reporter. His or her job is to type (in shorthand fashion—that's what the machine does) notes for a "transcript." A transcript is a written rendition of everything said in the courtroom. For your appeal, this person is the most important one to befriend. Unfortunately, he or she is also the hardest to know because he or she is constantly working on that little machine. (In some places, the more old-fashioned court reporters still take down testimony in shorthand notebooks; in other places, computers and tape recorders replace or supplement the court reporter.)

However it is taken down, if it's necessary to prepare a transcript later on, the court reporter will take his or her shorthand notes (or tapes or computer disks) and type out, and then edit, the question-and-answer format of the proceedings. This is the only way an appeals court can review what went on.

The court reporter is supposed to take everything down. If an objection is made to a question or an offered exhibit (sometimes called "proffered evidence"), the transcript will reflect the text of that objection and the judge's ruling on it. The court reporter even takes down those little side-bar conferences the jury doesn't hear. A record has to be made of side-bar conferences for the purposes of the appeal.

HOW APPEAL COURTS WORK

Some people have the mistaken impression that a case appealed to a higher court is retried all over. Except in rare circumstances, this does not happen. Appeals courts in the United States are courts "of record" rather than courts "of first impression." In other words, all the taking of testimony, all the offering of exhibits, objections, etc., is done in the trial court (or "lower court"). The appellate court (the "higher court") doesn't take any more testimony. It doesn't let you call any more witnesses. It will listen to your arguments (both oral and written), but nothing beyond that.

All the appellate court has to depend on is the transcript that the court reporter prepared, and the court file that the court clerk kept track of, along with the exhibits, both "received" and "refused." It is only from these items that the appeals court will make its decision. All these items taken together are the "record." It's this "record" that you should adequately "make" during your trial.

Since this book isn't about how to proceed with an appeal, we will not focus on what to do in the "higher" court. We will note only that your written arguments in that court will no doubt be contained in a writing known as a "brief." This document might not be "brief" at all; it can run to several dozens of pages. Your brief will refer to what went on in the "lower" court. It can only do this by pointing to (or referencing) particular items in this "record." That is why it's crucially important for you to get to know the court reporter, the court clerks and law clerks, and the other courtroom personnel, and understand how they function.

MAKING THE RECORD

Remember the court reporter's job during the trial—to type up the shorthand edition of the transcript as it's happening. You want him or her to do the best job he or she can. So it makes sense to let him or her do that job.

Court reporters constantly give lawyers and witnesses lots of instructions about what to do and not to do in the courtroom to make sure the record is accurate and honest. The most common of these instructions is not to talk at the same time as somebody else, such as the judge, a witness, opposing counsel, etc. The court reporter can't possibly record two people speaking at once. If he or she marks exhibits in your courtroom, don't talk while he or she is doing that. Just wait your turn—there's plenty of time to make your objection, state your argument, or ask your question.

Also, beware of talking too fast—the court reporter can't take that down either. Sometimes persons with an accent or who talk too softly are impossible to understand. Speak up, speak clearly, and speak in a dialect others can understand. Tell your witnesses to do the same. Sometimes, if an interpreter translates what a foreign-speaking witness is saying, the court reporter will be at a loss as to what or how much of the testimony to try to transcribe. Give him or her some extra latitude in handling that situation.

In all these instances, court reporters have a sort of inherent power from the judge to stand-up and announce a halt in the proceedings when they simply cannot transcribe what is being said. They can interrupt anybody—including the judge. When they do, the only thing you can do is stop, shut up, and let the judge decide how to continue. Try not to get too overwrought in the heat of battle. Baffling the court reporter is not a clever courtroom tactic.

THE OFFER OF PROOF

We've already been over why and how to keep an exhibit list, and how to make an objection to a question or an exhibit. Those things will show up in the record in the appellate court.

There is one more important thing that you should know how to do when "making the record." That is making an "offer of proof." What do you do when a judge sustains your opponent's objection to a question you asked? The jury won't hear the answer to the question, because the witness can't give an answer. What do you do when a judge refuses to let you make some kind of argument to the jury? The court reporter can't transcribe unspoken words. How do these things become part of the "record," so that the appeals court can later decide if the judge was correct in not allowing the question of argument?

Do you stop and just give up? Well, you might if the matter isn't important or there is some other way of asking the question or making the argument. There often is. If the matter is important, and there is no other way of convincing the judge to let that witness answer that question, you have to get the court reporter to somehow take down whatever it was that would have been said.

An offer of proof is simply telling the court (and the court reporter) something that isn't told to the jury. It is like the "refused" exhibit. That becomes part of "the record," although the jury never looks at it. So too, an objectionable question can be "answered" (in a fashion), if it's answered outside the presence of the jury, but in the presence of the court reporter.

Begin by politely telling the judge you want to make an "offer of proof" (and use those words). He or she might tell you to wait to do so until later, but the judge knows he or she is really skating on thin ice with the appellate court if he or she doesn't let you make the offer at some time. More often, the judge will have you approach the bench for what looks to be another sidebar conference.

When he says you can approach, go up to your sidebar area and say in your sidebar tone of voice, "Your Honor, if the witness were allowed to answer that question the answer would be such-and-so." That's it. Don't argue the objection all over. Don't tell the judge he or she is an idiot (there are more artful ways of doing that). Don't rattle on with another question or say something at sidebar the jury should be hearing. Make your offer and go back to your seat.

Sometimes at the sidebar, or later when the jury is out of the courtroom, the judge will direct the witness to answer the objectionable question. He or she will do that to confirm (or not) your version of what the answer would be. Sometimes he or she won't bother with that. Either way, it is not important who says it or who hears it—except the court reporter, so he or she can make the offer of proof a part of "the record." Now the appeals court can know the answer.

RELEASE PENDING APPEAL

The subject of release pending appeal is particularly confusing. Many people believe that, if you have a right to appeal to higher court (and you generally do), you shouldn't have to start serving a jail sentence until the appeals court has ruled against you. Other people believe it's ludicrous for someone to stall a sentence almost indefinitely, by beginning the interminable process of appeal that the American system of justice permits.

There is no right to release pending appeal. The trial judge decides that question, at least in the first instance. It depends how serious the offense is, what the sentence is, and how likely the defendant is to skip out on the sentence. That is much the same criteria the judge uses to decide if he or she is going to grant bail pending trial. If he or she grants a release, the judge might require the defendant to engage a bail bondsman to secure his or her attendance later.

If the trial judge rules against your release pending appeal, you can usually get a hearing on that subject in the appeals court. This "hearing" may be done only by submitting paperwork, but it's a hearing nonetheless. Still, it's a matter of discretion with that court to decide about your release pending appeal.

Does the wealthier defendant get released on appeal, while the poorer one goes directly to jail upon conviction? That is unfortunately sometimes the case. Sometimes the only way any release is had pending appeal, is when a defendant can pay a bail bondsman. Another common instance is where the defendant has something to lose by failing to show up to serve his or her sentence (such as his or her house or car). Those defendants are more likely to fall into the category of "wealthier" as opposed to "poorer."

POST TRIAL MOTIONS

To reach an appeals court, most states have a rule that a defendant must first ask the trial judge to reverse himself or herself on whatever points of law the defendant feels merit an appeal. This is done by making what is known as a "post trial motion." You go back to the judge who ruled against you in the first place, and ask him or her to admit to making a mistake. You say that he or she is wrong and should give you a new trial, this time doing things the right way (that is, your way).

Obviously, these motions very often fail. Judges, like everyone else, are never eager to admit they have made an error. The important point is not that you lose, it is that you complied with your local rule that says you have to go through the routine of asking the trial judge to correct himself or herself.

You can make a post trial motion for just about anything that went on in the courtroom. You can contend that evidence wasn't properly admitted and that led the jury to convict you. You can contend that evidence was refused that would have led the jury to acquit you. You can contend that your sentence was improperly issued, or is unduly harsh. You can claim that the prosecutor violated the standards of his or her noble office by treating you unfairly. You can even claim that the learned judge himself or herself had it in for you. If you think something went on in the courtroom that contributed to your defeat, make it part of a post trial motion.

Don't be too concerned about hurting someone's feelings. The people you will be insulting have already done as much to you as they are likely to do. When you bring a post trial motion, the judge will understand why you are doing it. Maybe if he or she sees you are serious about appealing the decision to his or her colleagues on the "higher" court, he or she might give your side of the case the serious attention it so obviously has always deserved.

Use the same format we suggested for pre-trial motions. Avoid trivial matters that no one really cares about. There are some *pro se* defendants (and some lawyers) who make motions, especially post trial motions, about every slight or irregularity that happens in court. Not only is it a waste of your time and the court's time in dealing with these, they are not going to impress the appellate court.

The rule of "harmless error" says that it's not enough to win on a particular point—winning the point has to make a difference. In other words, the appeals court may say, in effect, "It doesn't make any difference. The trial judge was wrong, but it's not a matter that had any bearing on guilt or the sentence imposed. It's a harmless error and the lower court decision stands."

Therefore, in this phase of your case, as in all phases, focus on what is important in your defense. Yes, you have to be careful and pay attention to details, especially since you are something of a stranger in this forest. But don't lose sight of the forest for the trees.

APPENDIX

I. *Substantive and Procedural Criminal Laws*

This part of the Appendix lists, state by state, where you can find the substantive and procedural criminal law applicable to your state.

Speaking generally, "substantive" criminal law concerns the kinds of crimes and their definitions discussed in Chapter 5. "Procedural" criminal law concerns the procedures that happen in the courtroom. For instance, if you wanted to see what distinguishes between first and second degree assault in your state, you would look under the substantive law. If you wanted to see what the next hearing was after the arraignment, you'd look under the procedural law.

Most large cities and county seats have a law library where you can find the actual text of these laws. They are sometimes, but not always, at local public libraries. You might have to call your city or county offices to find the nearest law library. If you ask the librarians there to help you find the books discussed here, they will generally be happy to help.

Because criminal law is largely a state by state matter, there are many variations in what each state calls it body of law. Finding the body of law you want can be very confusing. Let's start with the Federal sources of substantive and procedural law:

Jurisdiction	General & Substantive Law	Procedural Law
Federal	United States Code, Title 18- Crimes & Criminal Procedure	Federal Code of Criminal Procedure

Let's explain how the entries on this chart read. The above entry shows that the United States Government has a body of statutes called "United States Code." The term "statutes" means the book or books that contain acts passed by the legislature. At the federal level the legislature is the United States Congress. The United States Code is a multi-volume set of statutes. Some of those volumes are Title 18, which is entitled "Crimes and Criminal Procedure." It is in this section that you would find the federal law defining various offenses, which is its substantive law.

As the name of Title 18 suggests, you would probably also find a good deal of criminal procedure in those volumes. We have not repeated that entry under the "Procedural" law section, however. What is there is another strictly procedural body of law known as the Federal Code of Criminal Procedure. This is in addition to Title 18 and should be consulted for procedural questions as well.

Many states have followed this practice. The general distinction between the statutes and these procedural rules is that the latter have usually been enacted by some commission formed by the Legislature or state court system. The statutes themselves are enacted directly by the Legislature, like Title 18 of the United States Code. It is important to remember that not only may you find some procedural law mixed in with the substantive, but that the various codes of criminal procedural (and not every state has one) sometimes duplicate the statutes, sometimes overrule the statutes, and sometimes supplement them.

Let's go on to look at a state entry:

Jurisdiction	General & Substantive Law	Procedural Law
Alabama	Code of Alabama, Title 13 A- Criminal Code	Code of Alabama, Title 15 Criminal Procedure; and Alabama Rules of Criminal Procedure

As you can see, Alabama has a body of substantive criminal law—Title 13A. It also has a separate statute with criminal procedure in it—Title 15. Beyond that, it has another body of rules (the work of a commission as we said earlier) about criminal procedures. Again, the two sources of criminal procedural law should be read together.

In reviewing the statutes and rules of any state, you should also be aware that they are frequently updated, annually in some places. The general practice is to print a main edition of a state's statutes every few years, and to print annual supplements in a paper-bound volume known as the "pocket parts." Those "pocket parts" should be checked for recent developments.

Finally, be aware that this book also discusses some evidentiary rules that apply in criminal cases. The statutes cited here will show some of those special rules of evidence for criminal cases but not the general rules of evidence that come up in all cases, civil or criminal. Most states have yet another source of evidence law, usually entitled "Rules of Evidence." If you wind up checking on the criminal laws in your state, remember to keep these rules in mind for evidence questions.

The rest of our table:

Jurisdiction	Substantive	Procedure
Alaska	Alaska Statutes, Title 11-Criminal Law	Alaska Statutes, Title 12-Alaska Rules of Criminal Procedure
Arizona	Arizona Revised Statutes, Title 13-Arizona Criminal Code	Arizona Rules of Criminal Procedure
Arkansas in	Arkansas Code of 1987, Title 5-Criminal Offenses	Arkansas Code of 1987, Title 16-Practice and Procedure Courts, especially subtitle 6 Criminal Procedure Generally
California	California Penal Code, Part I-Crimes and Punishment	California Penal Code II-of Criminal Procedure and California Rules of Court
Colorado	Colorado Revised Statutes, Title 18-Criminal Code	Colorado Revised Statutes Title 16-Code of Criminal Procedure
Connecticut	Connecticut General Statutes, Title 53-Crimes	Connecticut General Statutes-Title 54-Criminal Procedure; and Connecticut Superior Court Rules, Sections 593 et seq.-Procedure in Criminal Cases

Jurisdiction	Substantive	Procedure
Delaware	Delaware Code Annotated, Title 11-Crimes or Criminal Procedure	
District of Columbia	D.C. Code, Title 22-Criminal Offenses	D.C. Code, Title 23-Criminal Procedure
Florida	Florida Statutes, Chapter 46 -Crimes	Florida Statutes, Chapter 47 -Criminal Procedure and Corrections; and Florida Rules of Criminal Procedure
Georgia	Offenses Code of Georgia, Title 16-Crimes	Offense Code of Georgia, Title 17-Criminal Procedure
Hawaii	Hawaii Revised Statutes, Title 37-Hawaii Penal Code	Hawaii Revised Statutes, Title 38-Procedural and Supplementary Provisions
Idaho	Idaho Code, Title 18-Crimes and Punishment	Idaho Code, Title 19 -Criminal Procedure and Idaho Criminal Rules
Illinois	Illinois Compiled Statutes, Chapter 720-Criminal Offenses	Illinois Compiled Statutes, Chapter 725-Criminal Procedure
Indiana	Indiana Code, Title 35-Criminal Law Procedure	
Iowa	Iowa Code, Title XVI (16)-Criminal Law Procedure, Sections 607 to 747	Iowa Code, Title XVI (16)-Criminal Law Procedure, Sections 801 et seq.
Kansas	Kansas Statutes, Chapter 21-Crimes and Punishments	Kansas Statutes, Chapter 22-Criminal Procedure; and Kansas Code of Criminal Procedure
Kentucky	Kentucky Revised Statutes, Title XL (40)-Crimes and Punishments	Kentucky Rules of Criminal Procedure
Louisiana	Louisiana Revised Statutes, Title 14-Criminal Law	Louisiana Revised Statutes, Title 15-Criminal Procedure
Maine	Maine Revised Statutes, Title 17-Crime	Maine Revised Statutes, Title 15-Court Procedure, Criminal; and Maine Rules of Criminal Procedure

Jurisdiction	Substantive	Procedure
Maryland	Code of Maryland, Article 27-Crimes and Punishment	Code of Maryland, Title 4-Criminal Causes; and Maryland Rules of Criminal Procedure
Massachusetts	Laws of Massachusetts, Part IV-Crimes, Punishment and Proceedings in Criminal Cases, Title 1-Crimes and Punishments	Laws of Massachusetts, Part IV-Crimes, Punishment and Proceedings in Criminal Cases, Title 2-Proceedings in Criminal Cases; and Massachusetts Rules of Criminal Procedure
Michigan	Michigan Compiled Laws, Code of Criminal Procedure, Chapter 760-776; Michigan Statutes Annotated,	Michigan Compiled Laws, Code of Criminal Procedure, Chapter 780-Criminal Procedure; and Michigan Court Rules of 1985
Minnesota	Minnesota Statutes, Section 609 -Criminal Code	Minnesota Rules of Criminal Procedure
Mississippi	Mississippi Code 1972, Title 97 Crimes	Mississippi Code 1972, Title 99-Criminal Procedure
Missouri	Vernon's Missouri Statutes, Title XXXVII (38)-Crimes and Punishments, Peace Officers and Public Defenders	Vernon's Missouri Statutes, Title XXXVII (37)-Criminal Procedure
Montana	Montana Code, Title 45-Crimes	Montana Code, Title 46-Criminal Procedure
Nebraska	Revised Statutes of Nebraska Chapter 28-Crimes and Punishments	Revised Statutes of Nebraska Chapter 29-Criminal Procedure
New Hampshire	New Hampshire Revised Statutes, Title LVIII (58)-Public Justice	New Hampshire Revised Statutes, Title LIX (59)-Proceedings in Criminal Cases
New Jersey	New Jersey Statutes, Title 2C -The New Jersey Code of Criminal Justice	New Jersey Statutes, Title 2A Administration of Criminal and Civil Justice, Subtitle 11 Criminal Procedure

Jurisdiction	Substantive	Procedure
New Mexico	New Mexico Statutes, Chapter 30-Criminal Offenses	New Mexico Statutes, Chapter 31-Criminal Procedure
New York	McKinney's Consolidated Laws of New York Annotated, Book 39-Penal Law	McKinney's Consolidated Laws of New York, Book 11A -Criminal Procedure Law
North Carolina	General Statues of North Carolina, Chapter 14-Criminal Law	General Statutes of North Carolina, Chapter 15-Criminal Procedure
North Dakota	North Dakota Century Code, Title 12.1-Criminal Code	North Dakota Century Code, Title 29-Judicial Procedures, Criminal; and North Dakota Rules of Criminal Procedure
Ohio	Page's Ohio Revised Code Annotated, Title 29-Criminal Crimes & Punishment	Ohio Rules of Criminal Procedure
Oklahoma	Oklahoma Statutes, Title 21-Crimes and Punishments	Oklahoma Statutes, Title 22-Criminal Procedure
Oregon	Oregon Revised Statutes, Title 16-Crimes and Punishments	Oregon Revised Statutes, Title 14-Procedure in Criminal Matters Generally; and Title 15-Procedure in Criminal Actions and Justices Court
Pennsylvania	Purdon's Pennsylvania Consolidated Statutes, Title -18-Crimes and Offenses	Purdon's Pennsylvania Consolidated Statutes Title 19 Criminal Procedure
Rhode Island	General Laws of Rhode Island, Title 11-Criminal Offenses	
South Carolina	Code of Laws of South Carolina, Title 16-Criminal Offenses	Code of Laws of South Carolina, Title 17-Criminal Procedure
South Dakota	South Dakota Codified Laws, Title 2-Crimes	South Dakota Codified Laws, Title 3A-Criminal Procedure

Jurisdiction	Substantive	Procedure
Tennessee	Tennessee Code, Title 39-Criminal Offenses	Tennessee Code, Title 40-Criminal Procedure; and Tennessee Rules of Criminal Procedure
Texas	Vernon's Texas Codes-Penal Code	Vernon's Texas Statutes, Article 1-Code of Criminal Procedure
Utah	Utah Code, Title 76-Criminal Code	Utah Code, Title 77-Code of Criminal Procedure
Vermont	Vermont Statutes, Title 13-Crimes and Criminal Procedure	
Virginia	Code of Virginia, Title 18-Crimes and Offenses Generally	Code of Virginia, Title 19-Criminal Procedure
Washington	Revised Code of Washington, Title 9-Crime and Punishments; and Title 9A-Washington Criminal Code	Revised Code of Washington, Title 10-Criminal Procedure
West Virginia	West Virginia Code, Chapter 61-Crimes and Their Punishment	West Virginia Code, Chapter 62-Criminal Procedure
Wisconsin	Wisconsin Statutes, Chapters Chapters 939-950-Criminal Code	Wisconsin Statutes, Chapters 967-979-Criminal Procedure
Wyoming	Wyoming Statutes, Title 6-Crimes and Offenses	Wyoming Statutes, Title 7-Criminal Procedure

II. Federal Sentencing Guidelines Grid

SENTENCING TABLE

(in months of imprisonment)

Criminal History Category (Criminal History Points)

Zone	Offense Level	I 0 or 1	II 2 or 3	III 4, 5, 6	IV 7, 8, 9	V 10, 11, 12	VI 13 or more
	1	0–6	0–6	0–6	0–6	0–6	0–6
	2	0–6	0–6	0–6	0–6	0–6	1–7
	3	0–6	0–6	0–6	0–6	2–8	3–9
	4	0–6	0–6	0–6	2–8	4–10	6–12
	5	0–6	0–6	1–7	4–10	6–12	9–15
	6	0–6	1–7	2–8	6–12	9–15	12–18
	7	0–6	2–8	4–10	8–14	12–18	15–21
A	8	0–6	4–10	6–12	10–16	15–21	18–24
	9	4–10	6–12	8–14	12–18	18–24	21–27
B	10	6–12	8–14	10–16	15–21	21–27	24–30
	11	8–14	10–16	12–18	18–24	24–30	27–33
C	12	10–16	12–18	15–21	21–27	27–33	30–37
D	13	12–18	15–21	18–24	24–30	30–37	33–41
	14	15–21	18–24	21–27	27–33	33–41	37–46
	15	18–24	21–27	24–30	30–37	37–46	41–51
	16	21–27	24–30	27–33	33–41	41–51	46–57
	17	24–30	27–33	30–37	37–46	46–57	51–63
	18	27–33	30–37	33–41	41–51	51–63	57–71
	19	30–37	33–41	37–46	46–57	57–71	63–78
	20	33–41	37–46	41–51	51–63	63–78	70–87

Zone	Offense Level	I 0 or 1	II 2 or 3	III 4, 5, 6	IV 7, 8, 9	V 10, 11, 12	VI 13 or more
	21	37–46	41–51	46–57	57–71	70–87	77–96
	22	41–51	46–57	51–63	63–78	77–96	84–105
	23	46–57	51–63	57–71	70–87	84–105	92–115
	24	51–63	57–71	63–78	77–96	92–115	100–125
	25	57–71	63–78	70–87	84–105	100–125	110–137
	26	63–78	70–87	78–97	92–115	110–137	120–150
	27	70–87	78–97	87–108	100–125	120–150	130–162
	28	78–97	87–108	97–121	110–137	130–162	140–175
	29	97–108	97–121	108–135	121–151	140–175	151–188
	30	97–121	108–135	121–151	135–168	151–188	168–210
	31	108–135	121–151	135–168	151–188	168–210	188–235
	32	121–151	135–168	151–188	168–210	188–235	210–262
	33	135–168	151–188	168–210	188–235	210–262	235–293
	34	151–188	168–210	188–235	210–262	235–293	262–327
	35	168–210	188–235	210–262	235–293	262–327	292–365
	36	188–235	210–262	235–293	262–327	292–365	324–405
	37	210–262	235–293	262–237	292–365	324–405	360–life
	38	235–293	262–327	292–365	324–405	360–life	360–life
	39	262–327	292–365	324–405	360–life	360–life	360–life
	40	292–365	324–405	360–life	360–life	360–life	360–life
	41	324–405	360–life	360–life	360–life	360–life	360–life
	42	360–life	360–life	360–life	360–life	360–life	360–life
	43	life	life	life	life	life	life

III. Common Form of Plea Agreement Used in Federal Court

UNITED STATES DISTRICT COURT

District of _____

_____ Division

Cr. No. _____

UNITED STATES OF AMERICA,	)	
Plaintiff,	)	
	)	PLEA AGREEMENT AND
vs.	)	SENTENCING GUIDELINES
	)	
JOHN DOE,	)	
Defendant.	)	

The United States by its Assistant United States Attorney, Jack Reno, and the defendant, John Doe, by himself, and with his attorney, Perry Mason, hereby agree to dispose of this case on the following terms and conditions pursuant to Rule 11 of the Federal Rules of Criminal Procedure and Section 6B1.4 of the Sentencing Guideline Manual of the United States Sentencing Commission.

PLEA AGREEMENT

The defendant and the government agree, pursuant to Rule 11, as follows:

1(a).   The defendant will plead guilty to Count I of the Superseding Indictment (II), charging conspiracy to distribute cocaine and cocaine base, also known as crack, in Minnesota in 1994 and until approximately February 3, 1995. It is stipulated and agreed that defendant aided Don Corleone to sell in excess of 50 grams of cocaine base pursuant to the conspiracy; and

1(b).   The defendant will plead guilty to Count XIII charging a money laundering offense, namely, his purchase and transfer of title of a 1993 Ford van knowingly using the proceeds of the unlawful activity, the sale of cocaine, and that the transaction was designed in part to conceal the nature, source, and ownership of the $3,000 in proceeds used.

2.   At the time of sentencing, if this plea agreement is accepted, the government will dismiss Counts XI and XII which are the remaining counts as to this defendant.

3(a).   This is a plea agreement entered into pursuant to the Rule 11(e)(1)(B) Fed.R.Crim.P. and U.S.S.G. Chapter 1, paragraph 4(c) and Section 6B1.2(b) for a recommendation of a specific sentence range of 30 to 36 months conditioned on the following terms. The defendant agrees to cooperate fully in the investigation and prosecution of other persons involved in the supply and distribution of cocaine and cocaine base into Minnesota, in the time period he was involved. He agrees he will give full and honest answers to questions asked. He has given interviews. He agrees he will testify fully and honestly before grand juries and at hearings and trials when requested to appear. The government agrees not to prosecute charges against the defendant based on evidence developed by this assistance.

3(b).   The government agrees to make a motion pursuant to 18 U.S.C. § 3553(e) and U.S.S.G. § 5K1.1 to enable the Court to depart from the guidelines and from the minimum mandatory penalty, if the defendant provides substantial assistance and testifies truthfully at hearings and at the trials of these others, when requested to appear, and the United States concludes that this meets the standards of the above provisions of the law. It will be in the discretion of the Court to evaluate the truthfulness, significance and usefulness of the testimony and to give the departure the Court determines.

4.   It is agreed that the guidelines place the base offense conduct for Count I at severity level 32, for this defendant. The government recommends there be a reduction of three levels for acceptance of responsibility, to level 29 (32–3 = 29). The defendant indicated his intent to plead guilty before trial preparation was required. The defendant appears to have given substantial honest, helpful assistance to the government; this is spoken of again, below. Whether there will be reduction for acceptance of responsibility shall be determined by the Court in its discretion. The severity level for County XIII is level 23. § 2S1.1(a)(2) and (b)(1). It is agreed that the two offenses grouped together as one under § 3D1.2 since the money laundering was one aspect of the overall cocaine distribution conspiracy and is an integral part of the aggregate harm. Therefore the guidelines level for Count I (above) is solely applicable. § 3D1.3. It is agreed that § 5G1.2 applies and therefore the sentences shall run together, concurrently.

5.   The criminal history category appears to be category I based on no criminal history points. If the court determines that the criminal history is higher than this, the guideline range for sentencing range will be adjusted up to match the reality of the situation.

6.   The guideline range for sentencing, from Chapter 5 of the guidelines, appears therefore to be 87–108 months if acceptance of responsibility is found. The defendant consents to placement in the shock incarceration problem (boot camp) under 18 U.S.C. § 4046. The government will not oppose a recommendation to that program (boot camp) if the Bureau of Prisons decides that the defendant becomes eligible. There is a minimum mandatory penalty of 10 years for an offense involving 50 grams or more of cocaine base (21 U.S.C. § 841(b)(1)(A)(iii). The motions under paragraph 3(b), above, enable the court to depart from this penalty. The maximum statutory penalty of imprisonment is life in prison. The actual guideline factors will be determined by the Court. The Court is not bound by this stipulation agreement. If the Court determines the factors to be different from those set forth here, the defendant will not be entitled to withdraw from the plea agreement.

7.   It shall be the judgment of the Court whether there shall be a fine. The statutory maximum is $4 million. The guideline range for fines is $15,000 to $150,000 as set forth at § 5E1.2(c)(3). The defendant has few assets.

8.   The applicable guideline supervised release term is 5 years. The statute sets forth a range of a minimum of 5 years and up to life supervised release. The defendant understands that, if he were to violate any condition of supervised release, he could be sentenced to an additional term of imprisonment up to the length of the original supervised release term. The term of supervised release may be extended to the maximum, during the term of supervised release.

9.   The defendant is liable to pay a special assessment of $50.00, pursuant to law, payable at the time of the plea.

10.   It is stipulated that Counts I and XIII of the indictment are true and correct and that the defendant is guilty of those offenses. The indictment is incorporated herein by reference. The defendant at various times in 1994 and 1995 agreed, actually and implicitly, with persons named there to distribute cocaine base in Minnesota, and took steps to carry out the agreement, including several distributions of crack cocaine; and the defendant knowingly purchased a 1993 Ford conversion van in his own name for defendant Don Corleone using in part $3,000 of proceeds of Corleone's drug sales to assist Corleone conceal the ownership and control of the proceeds as charged.

11.   Both parties waive their right to appeal the sentence imposed if the court accepts the sentencing range in paragraph 3(a).

12.   It is clearly and fully agreed that the guilty plea pursuant to this agreement is a final resolution upon the issue of guilt.

Dated: _____   United States Attorney

_____

By: Jack Reno
Assistant U.S. Attorney
Attorney ID Number: _____

Dated: _____   _____

John Doe
Defendant

Dated: _____   _____

Perry Mason
Attorney for Defendant
Attorney ID Number: _____

IV. Common Courtroom Objections

Phrase your objection by starting "Objection, Your Honor". Then continue with a combination of a **Form of Objection** (A or B or C) from the list below, plus one of the **Grounds For Objection** (1-11) in the table below that. Match up the grounds with the form through the headings at the top of the table of grounds.

Note that Objection A is directed to the form of your opponent's question. Objection B is directed at the answer which your opponent's question calls for. Objection C is made after the question has been asked and answered; if your objection is sustained, the judge should also instruct the jury to disregard the answer.

So you could make Objection A2 to the question this way, "Objection, Your Honor, the question is argumentative". You could make much the same objection to an argumentative answer with Objection B2 or C2. But you can only object, "Objection, Your Honor, the question is suggestive" with Objection A2, since only the question can be objected to on these grounds—you can't object that an answer is suggestive.

This form is all you have to say. If your judge wants more extensive argument about the objection, wait for him to ask for it.

Form of Objection

A.   The question is _____ .

B.   The question calls for an answer which is _____ .

C.   The answer is _____ ; also, I move to strike and ask the court to instruct the jury to disregard the answer.

Grounds For Objection

	A, B, C	B, C	A	C	A, C
1.	Improper	Incompetent	Leading	Not Responsive	Rambling
2.	Argumentative	Immaterial	Suggestive	Evasive	
3.	Compound	Irrelevant Multiplicitous	Defective in form		
4.	Repetitious	Speculative			
5.	Of no probative value	Opinion testimony			
6.	Ambiguous and uncertain	Hearsay			
7.	Misleading to the witness (or jury)	For which no predicate has been laid			
8.	Not supported by the pleadings	As not the best evidence			
9.	Collateral to the issue	Confidential and privileged a. husband/wife b. attorney/client c. physician/patient d. priest/penitent e. accountant/client f. informant g. psychotherapist /patient			
10.	Beyond the scope of proper cross (or direct) examination	Assumes facts not in evidence			
11.		Too general -opens too great of a field			

INDEX

personal recognizance bond, 39
petit misdemeanors. *See* misdemeanors
pharmaceutical, 52–53
phone call (one), 21–22
phone monitoring devices, 137
phone tap, 81
photographs, 85, 121, 123
photometric device. *See* breath analyzer
physical evidence. *See* evidence, physical
plea, 75, 91–93, 164–166; agreement, 92–93,
        164–165; bargain, 89, 125; deal, 92–94;
        negotiations, 56, 58, 76, 89–94, 135; petition,
        92–93
pleading, 89–90, 94, 96, 168
police, 10, 12–14, 17–33, 35–36, 38, 41, 47, 52–53,
        60, 64, 67–69, 80–82, 86, 95, 99, 104,
        110–11, 117, 119–20; brutality, 19; reports, 76
possession, 32, 52–54, 112
post-sentencing relief, 138
prejudices, 84, 123
preliminary breath test, 64
preliminary hearing, 76–77
pre-sentence investigation (PSI), 133–134, 136, 140
pretrial, 40
private attorney, 58–59
probable cause, 21, 23–24, 26–31, 76–77, 80;
        hearing, 76–77
probation, 40, 60, 135–40
probation office, 40, 90, 133–34, 140
procedural law, 55, 108
process server, 112–13
professional witness. *See* witness
proffered evidence. *See* evidence
property crimes, 48–50
prosecution, 15, 32, 36–37, 56–57, 76–77, 81–87,
        91, 95–96, 98, 100, 107–11, 113, 118–19,
        128–30, 141, 164
prosecution rests, 128
prosecution witness. *See* witness
prosecutor, 14, 32, 35–36, 58–60, 70, 76–78,
        81–83, 85–87, 89–95, 98, 101–103, 105, 107,
        109–18, 122–39, 131, 145, 153
pro se defendant, 63, 93, 103, 113, 153
prostitution, 54
PSI. *See* pre-sentence investigation
public defender, 38, 59
public drunkenness, 52, 54
public nuisance, 52

R

radar, 63, 68–73
rape, 44, 46, 50–51
receiving and concealing stolen property, 50
rehabilitation, 139

released on personal recognizance, 37
resisting arrest, 19, 21, 27, 51
restitution, 137, 140
robbery, 44, 48, 50

S

sandpaper, 111
scientific evidence. *See* evidence, scientific
scientific tests, 63, 65, 70, 72–73, 78, 86
scientific witness. *See* witness
searches and seizures, 23–27, 33, 78, 80–81, 85
search warrant. *See* warrant
second degree manslaughter. *See* manslaughter
second degree murder. *See* murder
seizure, 26, 33, 81
sentence, 20, 45, 52, 90, 92–93, 96, 130, 133–40,
        143, 151–53, 164–66; executed, 139; good
        time, 137; negotiations, 90; stayed, 139
sentencing grid, 136, 162
sentencing guidelines, 134, 136, 139, 162, 164
sequestration of witnesses, 82
severing the trial, 83
sex crimes, 50–51
sheriff, 18, 35, 99, 107, 112, 144
sidebar, 73, 127, 147–48, 150–51
simple misdemeanors. *See* misdemeanors
Sixth Amendment, 57–58
Star Chamber, 9–10
State Bureau of Criminal Apprehension, 10
statements, 14, 78–79, 81, 85, 110, 116–118,
        125–126, 129,
state penitentiary, 46, 137–38
state rests, 128
state's attorney, 12, 35
statutes, 22, 65, 92, 136
stool pigeon, 11
stop and frisk, 26
subpoena, 15, 72, 93, 112–13; power, 112; quashed,
        113
substantive law, 55
summation, 129
summons, 19, 35, 37–38
supervised release, 40, 165
support staff, 36
Supreme Court, 13, 24
surveillance, 81

T

tab charge, 20
target range, 68, 71
target tracking history, 69
tax violations, 51
testify, 9, 11, 22, 82, 86, 109–11, 113–14, 117–18,

Your #1 Source for Real World Legal Information...

LEGAL SURVIVAL GUIDES™

• Written by lawyers
• Simple English explanation of the law
• Forms and instructions included

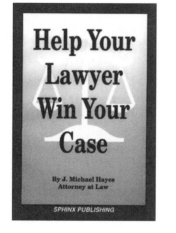

LEGAL RESEARCH MADE EASY

This book for non-lawyers explains how to use the various types of legal reference books such as legal encyclopedias, statutes, digests, American Law Reports, and Shepard's Citations, as well as computerized legal databases. Includes state and federal materials.

124 pages; $14.95;
ISBN 1-57248-008-4

HELP YOUR LAWYER WIN YOUR CASE

Even with a lawyer, what you know may determine whether you win or lose, and how much it will cost you. This book shows you how to save money, and help win your case. Topics include: selecting a lawyer, giving your lawyer good information, asking the right questions, understanding the system, and helping your lawyer prepare your case.

156 pages; $12.95;
ISBN 1-57248-021-1

LEGAL MALPRACTICE

Find out if you have a legitimate complaint against your lawyer, and if so, what you can do about it. Learn about your lawyer's ethical and legal duties, assessing your damages, suing your lawyer, Bar Association grievances, arbitration and mediation.

224 pages; $18.95;
ISBN 1-57248-032-7

What our customers say about our books:

"It couldn't be more clear for the lay person." —R.D.

"I want you to know I really appreciate your book. It has saved me a lot of time and money." —L.T.

"Your real estate contracts book has saved me nearly $12,000.00 in closing costs over the past year." —A.B.

"...many of the legal questions that I have had over the years were answered clearly and concisely through your plain English interpretation of the law." —C.E.H.

"If there weren't people out there like you I'd be lost. You have the best books of this type out there." —S.B.

"...your forms and directions are easy to follow." —C.V.M.

Legal Survival Guides are directly available from the publisher, or from your local bookstores.
For credit card orders call 1–800–43–BRIGHT, write P.O. Box 372, Naperville, IL 60566,
or fax 630-961-2168

Legal Survival Guides™ National Titles
Valid in All 50 States

Legal Survival in Business

How to Form Your Own Corporation (2E)	$19.95
How to Register Your Own Copyright (2E)	$19.95
How to Register Your Own Trademark (2E)	$19.95
Most Valuable Business Forms You'll Ever Need	$19.95
Most Valuable Corporate Forms You'll Ever Need	$24.95
Software Law (with diskette)	$29.95

Legal Survival in Court

Crime Victim's Guide to Justice	$19.95
Debtors' Rights (2E)	$12.95
Defend Yourself Against Criminal Charges	$19.95
Grandparents' Rights	$19.95
Help Your Lawyer Win Your Case	$12.95
Jurors' Rights	$9.95
Legal Malpractice and Other Claims Against Your Lawyer	$18.95
Legal Research Made Easy	$14.95
Simple Ways to Protect Yourself From Lawsuits	$24.95
Victim's Rights	$12.95
Winning Your Personal Injury Claim	$19.95

Legal Survival in Real Estate

How to Buy a Condominium or Townhome	$16.95
How to Negotiate Real Estate Contracts (2E)	$16.95
How to Negotiate Real Estate Leases (2E)	$16.95
Successful Real Estate Brokerage Management	$19.95

Legal Survival in Personal Affairs

How to File Your Own Bankruptcy (4E)	$19.95
How to File Your Own Divorce (3E)	$19.95
How to Make Your Own Will	$12.95
How to Write Your Own Living Will	$9.95
Living Trusts and Simple Ways to Avoid Probate	$19.95
Neighbor vs. Neighbor	$12.95
Power of Attorney Handbook (2E)	$19.95
Social Security Benefits Handbook	$14.95
U.S.A. Immigration Guide (2E)	$19.95
Guia de Inmigracion a Estados Unidos	$19.95

Legal Survival Guides are directly available from the publisher, or from your local bookstores.

For credit card orders call 1–800–43–BRIGHT, write P.O. Box 372, Naperville, IL 60566, or fax 630-961-2168

LEGAL SURVIVAL GUIDES™ STATE TITLES
Up-to-date for Your State

NEW YORK

How to File for Divorce in NY	$19.95
How to Make a NY Will	$12.95
How to Start a Business in NY	$16.95
How to Win in Small Claims Court in NY	$14.95
Landlord's Rights and Duties in NY	$19.95
New York Power of Attorney Handbook	$12.95

PENNSYLVANIA

How to File for Divorce in PA	$19.95
How to Make a PA Will	$12.95
How to Start a Business in PA	$16.95
Landlord's Rights and Duties in PA	$19.95

FLORIDA

Florida Power of Attorney Handbook	$9.95
How to Change Your Name in FL (3E)	$14.95
How to File a FL Construction Lien (2E)	$19.95
How to File a Guardianship in FL	$19.95
How to File for Divorce in FL (4E)	$21.95
How to Form a Nonprofit Corp in FL (3E)	$19.95
How to Form a Simple Corp in FL (3E)	$19.95
How to Make a FL Will (4E)	$9.95
How to Modify Your FL Divorce Judgement (3E)	$22.95
How to Probate an Estate in FL (2E)	$24.95
How to Start a Business in FL (4E)	$16.95
How to Win in Small Claims Court in FL (5E)	$14.95
Land Trusts in FL (4E)	$24.95
Landlord's Rights and Duties in FL (6E)	$19.95
Women's Legal Rights in FL	$19.95

GEORGIA

How to File for Divorce in GA (2E)	$19.95
How to Make a GA Will (2E)	$9.95
How to Start and Run a GA Business (2E)	$18.95

ILLINOIS

How to File for Divorce in IL	$19.95
How to Make an IL Will	$9.95
How to Start a Business in IL	$16.95

MASSACHUSETTS

How to File for Divorce in MA	$19.95
How to Make a MA Will	$9.95
How to Probate an Estate in MA	$19.95
How to Start a Business in MA	$16.95
Landlord's Rights and Duties in MA	$19.95

MICHIGAN

How to File for Divorce in MI	$19.95
How to Make a MI Will	$9.95
How to Start a Business in MI	$16.95

MINNESOTA

How to File for Divorce in MN	$19.95
How to Form a Simple Corporation in MN	$19.95
How to Make a MN Will	$9.95
How to Start a Business in MN	$16.95

NORTH CAROLINA

How to File for Divorce in NC	$19.95
How to Make a NC Will	$9.95
How to Start a Business in NC	$16.95

TEXAS

How to File for Divorce in TX	$19.95
How to Form a Simple Corporation in TX	$19.95
How to Make a TX Will	$9.95
How to Probate an Estate in TX	$19.95
How to Start a Business in TX	$16.95
How to Win in Small Claims Court in TX	$14.95
Landlord's Rights and Duties in TX	$19.95

Legal Survival Guides are directly available from the publisher, or from your local bookstores.

For credit card orders call 1–800–43–BRIGHT, write P.O. Box 372, Naperville, IL 60566, or fax 630-961-2168

Legal Survival Guides™ • Order Form

BILL TO:		SHIP TO:	
Phone #	**Terms**	**F.O.B.** Chicago, IL	**Ship Date**

Charge my:

VISA ☐ VISA MasterCard ☐ Mastercard AMERICAN EXPRESS ☐ American Express

☐ **Money Order** (no personal checks please)

Credit Card Number **Expiration Date**

Qty	ISBN	Title	Retail
		Legal Survival Guides Fall 97 National Frontlist	
	1-57071-223-9	How to File Your Own Bankruptcy (4E)	$19.95
	1-57071-224-7	How to File Your Own Divorce (3E)	$19.95
	1-57071-227-1	How to Form Your Own Corporation (2E)	$19.95
	1-57071-228-X	How to Make Your Own Will	$12.95
	1-57071-225-5	How to Register Your Own Copyright (2E)	$19.95
	1-57071-226-3	How to Register Your Own Trademark (2E)	$19.95
		Fall 97 New York Frontlist	
	1-57071-184-4	How to File for Divorce in NY	$19.95
	1-57071-183-6	How to Make a NY Will	$12.95
	1-57071-185-2	How to Start a Business in NY	$16.95
	1-57071-187-9	How to Win in Small Claims Court in NY	$14.95
	1-57071-186-0	Landlord's Rights and Duties in NY	$19.95
	1-57071-188-7	New York Power of Attorney Handbook	$12.95
		Fall 97 Pennsylvania Frontlist	
	1-57071-177-1	How to File for Divorce in PA	$19.95
	1-57071-176-3	How to Make a PA Will	$12.95
	1-57071-178-X	How to Start a Business in PA	$16.95
	1-57071-179-8	Landlord's Rights and Duties in PA	$19.95
		Legal Survival Guides National Backlist	
	1-57071-166-6	Crime Victim's Guide to Justice	$19.95
	1-57248-023-8	Debtors' Rights (2E)	$12.95
	1-57071-162-3	Defend Yourself Against Criminal Charges	$19.95
	1-57248-001-7	Grandparents' Rights	$19.95
	0-913825-99-9	Guia de Inmigracion a Estados Unidos	$19.95
	1-57248-021-1	Help Your Lawyer Win Your Case	$12.95
	1-57071-164-X	How to Buy a Condominium or Townhome	$16.95
	1-57248-035-1	How to Negotiate Real Estate Contracts (2E)	$16.95
	1-57248-036-X	How to Negotiate Real Estate Leases (2E)	$16.95
	1-57071-167-4	How to Write Your Own Living Will	$9.95
	1-57248-031-9	Jurors' Rights	$9.95
	1-57248-032-7	Legal Malpractice and Other Claims Against Your Lawyer	$18.95
	1-57248-008-4	Legal Research Made Easy	$14.95
	1-57248-019-X	Living Trusts and Simple Ways to Avoid Probate	$19.95
	1-57248-022-X	Most Valuable Business Forms You'll Ever Need	$19.95
	1-57248-007-6	Most Valuable Corporate Forms You'll Ever Need	$24.95
	0-913825-41-7	Neighbor vs. Neighbor	$12.95
	1-57248-044-0	Power of Attorney Handbook (2E)	$19.95
	1-57248-020-3	Simple Ways to Protect Yourself From Lawsuits	$24.95
	1-57248-033-5	Social Security Benefits Handbook	$14.95
	1-57071-163-1	Software Law (w/diskette)	$29.95
	0-913825-86-7	Successful Real Estate Brokerage Mgmt.	$19.95
	1-57248-000-9	U.S.A. Immigration Guide (2E)	$19.95
	0-913825-82-4	Victim's Rights	$12.95
	1-57071-165-8	Winning Your Personal Injury Claim	$19.95
		Florida Backlist	
	0-913825-81-6	Florida Power of Attorney Handbook	$9.95
	1-57248-028-9	How to Change Your Name in FL (3E)	$14.95
	0-913825-84-0	How to File a FL Construction Lien (2E)	$19.95
	0-913825-53-0	How to File a Guardianship in FL	$19.95
	1-57248-046-7	How to File for Divorce in FL (4E)	$21.95

Qty	ISBN	Title	Retail
		Florida Backlist (cont')	
	1-57248-004-1	How to Form a Nonprofit Corp in FL (3E)	$19.95
	0-913825-96-4	How to Form a Simple Corp in FL (3E)	$19.95
	1-57248-027-0	How to Make a FL Will (4E)	$9.95
	1-57248-056-4	How to Modify Your FL Divorce Judgement (3E)	$22.95
	1-57248-003-3	How to Probate an Estate in FL (2E)	$24.95
	1-57248-005-X	How to Start a Business in FL (4E)	$16.95
	0-913825-97-2	How to Win in Small Claims Court in FL (5E)	$14.95
	1-57248-029-7	Land Trusts in FL (4E)	$24.95
	1-57248-057-2	Landlord's Rights and Duties in FL (6E)	$19.95
	0-913825-73-5	Women's Legal Rights in FL	$19.95
		Georgia Backlist	
	1-57248-058-0	How to File for Divorce in GA (2E)	$19.95
	1-57248-047-5	How to Make a GA Will (2E)	$9.95
	1-57248-026-2	How to Start and Run a GA Business (2E)	$18.95
		Illinois Backlist	
	1-57248-042-4	How to File for Divorce in IL	$19.95
	1-57248-043-2	How to Make an IL Will	$9.95
	1-57248-041-6	How to Start a Business in IL	$16.95
		Massachusetts Backlist	
	1-57248-051-3	How to File for Divorce in MA	$19.95
	1-57248-050-5	How to Make a MA Will	$9.95
	1-57248-053-X	How to Probate an Estate in MA	$19.95
	1-57248-054-8	How to Start a Business in MA	$16.95
	1-57248-055-6	Landlord's Rights and Duties in MA	$19.95
		Michigan Backlist	
	1-57248-014-9	How to File for Divorce in MI	$19.95
	1-57248-015-7	How to Make a MI Will	$9.95
	1-57248-013-0	How to Start a Business in MI	$16.95
		Minnesota Backlist	
	1-57248-039-4	How to File for Divorce in MN	$19.95
	1-57248-040-8	How to Form a Simple Corporation in MN	$19.95
	1-57248-037-8	How to Make a MN Will	$9.95
	1-57248-038-6	How to Start a Business in MN	$16.95
		North Carolina Backlist	
	0-913825-94-8	How to File for Divorce in NC	$19.95
	0-913825-92-1	How to Make a NC Will	$9.95
	0-913825-93-X	How to Start a Business in NC	$16.95
		Texas Backlist	
	0-913825-91-3	How to File for Divorce in TX	$19.95
	1-57248-009-2	How to Form a Simple Corporation in TX	$19.95
	0-913825-89-1	How to Make a TX Will	$9.95
	1-57248-010-6	How to Probate an Estate in TX	$19.95
	0-913825-90-5	How to Start a Business in TX	$16.95
	1-57248-012-2	How to Win in Small Claims Court in TX	$14.95
	1-57248-011-4	Landlord's Rights and Duties in TX	$19.95
		SUBTOTAL	
		IL Residents add 6.75%, FL Residents add county sales tax	
		Shipping— $4.00 for 1st book, $1.00 each additional	
		Total	

To order, call Sourcebooks at 1-800-43-BRIGHT or FAX (630)961-2168 (Bookstores, libraries, wholesalers—please call for discount)